HOW TO SUCCEED IN SECONDARY SCHOOL

A Practical Guide

TONY BELLEW

ORPEN PRESS

Published by
Orpen Press
Upper Floor, Unit B3
Hume Centre
Hume Avenue
Park West Industrial Estate
Dublin 12

email: info@orpenpress.com
www.orpenpress.com

Paperback ISBN 978-1-78605-120-2
ePub ISBN 978-1-78605-121-9

Printed in Dublin by SPRINTprint Ltd

This book is dedicated to my family – my wife, Cree; daughters, Karen and Stacey; son, Andrew; and grandchildren, Sophie, Bailey, Elliot, Cameron, Dillon, Romy, Stella and Spencer. Also, my sons-in-law, Robbie and Patrick; and my daughter-in-law, Louise.

About the Author

Tony Bellew was educated at Presentation College, Bray and University College Dublin. Having qualified as a secondary school teacher, he spent 38 years in St Brendan's College, Woodbrook, Bray (now Woodbrook College). For the first 20 years, he taught Business Studies to Intermediate Certificate students (later known as Junior Certificate students) and Accounting, Economics and Business to Leaving Certificate students. He undertook many roles in middle management during his time there including year head and dean of discipline. He was appointed deputy principal in 2001 and principal in 2003. He served as principal for six years until his retirement in 2009. He served on the Board of Management from 1994 until 2009. On his retirement, he set up a one-to-one mentoring service for secondary school students.

He has worked with a large number of students over the past thirteen years offering help and advice on all aspects of their secondary school lives. He has also made numerous presentations to students and parents in a wide variety of secondary schools during this time. He was Chair of the Board of Management in Arklow CBS from 2009 to 2012. He was also appointed Chair of the Board of Management in Presentation College, Bray in 2012. He spent nine years in that role from 2012 until 2021.

He has been actively involved in rugby all of his life. He qualified as an IRFU coach in 1997 and has held a number of coaching roles at all levels. He introduced rugby to St Brendan's College in 1975 and coached the senior team there for the following 25 years.

Foreword

Foreword

This is an important and very timely publication. *How to Succeed in Secondary School: A Practical Guide* will be of great value to all second-level students, and in particular to senior cycle students and their parents, as well as teachers.

Having spent my professional career in second-level education, I am well placed to judge the merits of this impressive book. My experiences as class teacher, deputy principal and school principal have given me a clear insight into the challenges students face and how each individual student must forge a pathway through the complexities of their own lives outside the school community. Many students struggle to organise study effectively at home and at the same time cope with the various demands on their time. This publication and the process outlined therein provide a clear, tangible, balanced approach that overcomes these obstacles and produces consistently outstanding outcomes for students.

I have known the author, Tony Bellew, for thirty years and have worked closely with him in professional settings for the past fifteen years. He is an extremely dedicated individual who has contributed greatly to the school I worked in for over forty years. Tony was chairperson of the board of management for nine years and was an exemplary leader during that time. This is an all-consuming, voluntary role and Tony embraced all the challenges presented with passion, integrity, dedication and humanity.

Tony also provides mentoring support to our Leaving Certificate students. This support mirrors the streamlined, planned, systematic process outlined by Tony in his book, and has proven invaluable to our students over the years.

The relevance of this publication to students, parents, and indeed teachers and year heads, cannot be overstated. At a period of major educational changes in national educational policy and a time of unprecedented stress, uncertainty and confusion for our young people, Tony provides a clear roadmap to success and achievement in examinations that is personalised for each individual student. Tony's book guides the student through the process in an organised, structured and balanced manner that allows great scope for review and reflection.

Drawing on fifty years of diverse involvement in second-level education, Tony takes us through a systematic process that will empower students to take ownership and control of study and schoolwork outside the school setting. It is an in-depth, insightful and innovative reflection on how best to build on the excellent work done in schools to help students achieve their potential.

While recognising schools as 'communities of learning', Tony also emphasises the importance of extending this concept to life outside schools. This book takes the reader through the careful planning needed to achieve the attainable goals of each student. There is a clear emphasis on structure, quality, a positive attitude and target-setting. Critical appraisal is a fundamental part of this approach and work-in-progress notebooks, examination notebooks, ongoing monitoring of progress and self-reflection reality checks are key elements in this process.

Tony recognises and highlights the importance of balance in terms of study, leisure time, family time, and rest and recovery. He has also developed bespoke daily timetables that ensure that each student can function and achieve their best possible outcomes. Furthermore, he has devised three schedules of work that guide the student through normal school days, weekends, and midterms and holidays.

Of particular interest is the chapter dealing with the Leaving Certificate through the eyes of a student. The voice of the student is clearly heard as she outlines the impact Tony had on her journey throughout the year. She takes the reader through her journey and talks about the confidence and belief she gained from going through the process. The structure, planning, advice and kindness from Tony provided the springboard for the student to attain her goals. This concept really works! This book truly supplements and enhances the great work done in classrooms throughout the country.

Tony's experience and wisdom in the area of student achievement comes across very clearly throughout this book. His work and engagement with students in schools as well as his group and individual mentoring work outside school settings gives Tony huge credibility in this area. So too does the hugely impressive level of success he has had with so many students over the years. Tony Bellew is an authority on how best to organise and motivate students to fulfil their potential.

Throughout his career, Tony Bellew has been an advocate for young people. Through his work in school, as a sports coach and as an educational mentor, he has unparalleled expertise in the area of how best to motivate and organise students to reach their potential. He is a consummate professional who cares passionately about education and student learning. This book is an essential read and should be used to guide, advise and support every second-level student.

Pat Gregory
Former principal of Presentation College, Bray, Co. Wicklow

Preface

I have been looking at bringing real structure to students' lives for a long time now. It goes as far back as very early on in my teaching career. I particularly remember having large numbers in my Accounting and Economics class groups. I would have loved to have been able to spend time with my students in relation to this. Of course, this was never possible because of the very busy nature of secondary-school life. Even going back more than 30 years, I was determined to do something about this when the opportunity arose. My personal life was very busy too with a young family, a part-time job and my involvement in rugby. The opportunity to do something about this didn't come until my retirement in 2009. The word 'retirement' only applies to my role as principal of St Brendan's College. I was always going to continue working with students because of my deep passion for everything associated with them.

When I retired in 2009, my main focus was on bringing real structure to the lives of students outside of school. Everything is organised so well for them in school, I was determined to bring the same kind of structure to all aspects of each student's life outside of school. This involved working closely with them to design and manage their own schedule outside of school. My work assists them in taking responsibility for their own self-management.

I have said many times that I love 'busy' students. From this I mean that I love students to have interests outside of their school-related work. I am a great believer in making sure that there is good balance in each student's life. All leisure activities can be accommodated with good planning. The busier the student, the better, as far as I am concerned. I help students to bring the qualities/skills they have in other areas of their lives to enrich their school-related work.

I insist that each student I work with has a specific daily timetable for doing their homework, study and revision. A lot of planning and thought must go into this. It can take a lot of tweaking early on but, eventually, you get the timetable that suits best. Again, it is not written in stone. It can be altered to suit changing circumstances. Some students can be a little reluctant at first to take on board something like this. It takes commitment and students need to give it a chance. Once they settle in to it, most students become very comfortable with it. It gives them confidence as they know they have a set-up in place that gives them the best chance of succeeding. I believe that it is all about consistency through the year.

I have developed this concept over the past thirteen years to the point where I feel it is very close to being the finished article. There is a big emphasis on making the quality of work the best it can be at all times, becoming confident about performing to one's potential in examinations, dealing with difficulties/problems that students have to face, coping with set-backs and many more aspects. There are many examples of work schedules throughout the book. Also, the journey of a Sixth-Year student through her Leaving Certificate year is told by way of reports from our meetings.

My objective for each student is to be able to say: 'When I walk out of the last exam in the Leaving and Junior Certificate, I can look back knowing that I couldn't have done any more.' If this happens, you have given yourself every chance of realising your potential and achieving your targeted grade in each subject.

Contents

Chapter 1

Bringing Structure to Everything

Throughout my career in second-level education, I have always felt that there was never enough time to focus on students' lives outside of school. Secondary school life is just too busy for such interaction to take place on any regular basis. This is not a criticism of what goes on in secondary schools, it is just the way things are. From my early days as a teacher, I would regularly notice students who were not reaching their potential. I would have loved to have been able to offer one-to-one assistance to them but it was simply not possible. I recognised that students experience difficulties with many aspects of their lives outside of school in relation to school-related matters. The service they receive during normal school time is second to none. However, students can struggle a lot with areas of school-related work outside of normal classes. This can include organising or planning their homework, study and revision schedules both at supervised study in school or at home. They can also experience difficulty with making sure their work is of a high enough quality on a consistent basis. In addition, many students feel intimidated by tests/examinations and, as a result, don't do themselves justice in such situations. These are just a few of the areas I have focused on to help each individual student realise their potential as they negotiate their way through secondary school life.

> **Note:** Students must bring the same type of structure to their lives outside of school as is in place for them in school.

What This Book Is Trying to Achieve

The book focuses on all aspects of a student's life outside of what goes on in school. The service provided throughout secondary school life in each school is generally excellent. Students must make sure that all other aspects of their lives that will influence their progress will reach the same high standards. Everything in school is organised for them in a very efficient and organised way. This book will illustrate how best to get organised at home.

The book is mainly directed at Leaving Certificate students and their parents. A lot of the content is also appropriate for earlier years in secondary school and particular reference is made to First- and Third-Year students. The purpose of the book is to advise and support Sixth-Year students in relation to how to realise their potential in the Leaving Certificate examinations. For Third-Year students it will assist with regard to realising their potential in the Junior Certificate examination. And for First-, Second- and Fifth-Year students it will provide advice and support with regard to the end-of-year house examinations.

I have a huge amount of experience behind me. I spent 38 years in St Brendan's College, Bray (now Woodbrook College), experiencing all areas of second-level education from being a student teacher up to being principal of the college. I have spent the last thirteen years working with students on a one-to-one basis regarding all aspects of their lives outside of school. During this time, I have listened to the students I have worked with and have taken on board all of their concerns. I am passionate about the work I do with them. I take a personal interest in each student I work with. No two students are the same so a unique individual plan must be drawn up for each student. I firmly believe that every student can realise their potential with the right individual plan in place.

I have huge admiration for what goes on in secondary schools. I felt this through all of my 38-year career in St Brendan's and during the last thirteen years during which I have been a chairperson of boards of management (BOM). I have been Chairperson of the BOM of Presentation College, Bray for the last nine years. I have had a really 'hands-on' role there working closely with senior management and teachers on various initiatives. My involvement there has reinforced my admiration for the great work that goes on in our secondary schools. In fact, I believe that perhaps we are in danger of doing too much for students at times. My role now is to help the students I work with to achieve the results they are capable of by supporting themselves in a sustainable manner.

I have very strong views on certain key aspects in relation to them preparing for and performing in examinations. I can best explain a lot of this by going through all of the key elements of my 'One2One' mentoring service. This will highlight how each student should approach each year in secondary school and the key elements they must focus on. There is an emphasis on Sixth Year in particular, but much of the information applies to the other years as well.

Key areas that are focused on when drawing up an overall plan

- **Critical assessment of where each student is starting from:** This involves a very honest look at where the student is starting from at a particular point in time. Everything must be put on the table. This should be done at the start of the year. Then, the best plan can be put in place moving forward.
- **Assessment of performance to date:** This involves another very honest appraisal. Each student gives details of his commitment to his school-related work up until the current point. Again, this is done at the start of the year. This then makes it possible to put a realistic plan in place.
- **Setting of targets for the year:** This involves short-term, medium-term and long-term targets. The ultimate ones are the 'targeted grades' for all subjects in the Leaving and Junior Certificate examinations and, for other year groups, the house examinations at the end of the year. These are *outcomes*. We then must focus totally on the process involved in preparing for the examinations.

- **Making optimum use of breaks from school:** The breaks I refer to are the October mid-term break, the Christmas break, the February mid-term break and the Easter break. A big emphasis is put on having suitable plans in place for these. Examples of schedules for these breaks are provided for First-, Third- and Sixth-Year students.

- **Planning the 'Three Schedules of Work':** This is a huge part of the overall plan. Every effort is made to bring real structure to school-related work outside of school – a daily timetable for doing homework, study and revision. There are **three** main schedules of work – one for normal school days, one for weekends and one for mid-term breaks/holiday periods, etc. These form the basis of the plan for the year.

- **Facilitating leisure/sport/family/rest and recovery activities:** A huge emphasis is put on getting the balance right between school-related work and leisure/sport/family/rest and recovery activities. I put as much emphasis on this as I do on the work time. The leisure activities form a very important part of the overall plan.

- **Making the quality of homework, study and revision the best it can be:** Once the work schedules are in place, a big emphasis is put on making the quality of work the best it can be at all times. This is essential for satisfactory progress to be made. Students stand the best chance of realising their potential if their work is consistently of the required standard. I believe in taking care of the small details and – in my opinion – this leads to the big picture (the results in the examinations) taking care of itself.

- **Realising one's potential in examinations:** Many students can lack confidence when it comes to sitting exams. I have very strong views on how to prepare for exams. I call it becoming 'street wise' in relation to preparing for them. I have a handout on this with eighteen simple, basic points highlighted. Chapter 7 is totally devoted to this.

- **Stronger and weaker subjects:** Every student has stronger and weaker subjects. Usually, there are more strong ones. In relation to the strong ones, it is a matter of maintaining the high levels. In relation to weaker ones, it is a matter of working hard to become a little better. Again, I have very definite views in this regard. I don't accept that a student has to remain weak in a certain area. I have noticed, time and time again, that a student's 'weakest' subject may be the most important one in the Leaving Certificate. My theory is that the sixth subject counted for points is the most important one. If this one is prioritised and made as strong as it possibly can be, the ones above it will be at their strongest too. It might be the one that will bring you over the line, points wise, to gain entry into the course you really want. Hence, the importance of improving in your 'weaker' subjects. This theory applies to other year groups as well. If you can make your 'weaker' subjects as strong as they can be, all subjects will then be at the level you want.

- **Strengths and weaknesses:** I am referring here to strengths and weaknesses in our make-up. We must be determined to maintain the same high levels in relation to our strengths and strive to become better in the weaker areas. Typical weak areas would be laziness, poor concentration, being disorganised, lacking motivation, poor work ethic, etc. Once weaknesses have been identified, we must be determined to become a little better in each. A small improvement will add value to performance. Also, never take our strengths for granted. If we become complacent about them, standards will slip.

- **Developing a positive attitude to everything:** It is essential to adopt a positive attitude in relation to what you are trying to achieve. If you are negative about something, it is nearly impossible to succeed. I put a big emphasis on determination and commitment to succeed. My approach is: 'I am going to achieve my targets no matter what it takes.'

- **Having confidence in your ability to succeed:** Genuine confidence comes from hard work. Once the best plan is in place and each student commits to it, their confidence will grow as time moves on. They will begin to see that the plan is working and that progress is being made.

- **Coping with set-backs:** There are going to be set-backs through the journey. Each student has to be determined to succeed despite any obstacles they are confronted with. They must always look to find a way to deal with these. The attitude should be that 'nothing is going to stop me from achieving my goals.' Everything can be sorted out once you have a mindset to do it.

- **Monitoring progress on an ongoing basis**: It is one thing having a really good plan in place. But, each student must trust what is in place and commit totally to it. Then, we need to be sure that the plan is working. This comes by way of monitoring progress on a regular basis. Students must pay attention to class test results, comments from teachers, comments from parents, etc. Also, each student must be their own hardest critic.

- **Mock examinations:** I have very strong views on how to gain maximum benefit from the Mock examinations. This is covered in the 'Gaining Maximum Benefit from the Mocks' handout. The main points will be discussed in detail later.

- **Grinds:** Again, I have strong views on the use of these. Grinds should never be the be-all and end-all of everything. They should only be used as supplementary help. The primary source of information should always be formal classes in school. This is then followed by all the work/research, etc that each individual student does. If a student is still struggling, further help may be required which can come in the form of grinds. More about this later.

- **Identifying difficulties/problems and finding ways to address them:** When a difficulty/problem is identified, a way to sort it out must be found. The solution might be as simple as talking to a fellow student about the nature of the difficulty. Most difficulties can be sorted very easily. The important thing is that each student must be determined to find a way to sort it out and to do what is required.

- **'Work in progress' notebook:** This is something that I introduced a few years ago to help the students I work with. It is a simple way of temporarily parking important work that has to be done. I include here difficulties/problems that have to be sorted out. Items are listed and prioritised. It is checked regularly. Items are ticked off as they are attended to.

- **Examinations notebook:** It is used for class tests, house examinations and Mock examinations. It is all about learning from these for the Leaving and Junior Certificate examination. The emphasis is on where marks were lost. If a student gets 81%, I am more interested in the 19%. Identify why marks were lost and do whatever follow-up work is required so that marks like these won't be lost next time.

Chapter 2

The Leaving Certificate Year through the Eyes of a Student

This book looks at all aspects of a student's life outside of what goes on in school. Obviously, there is a big emphasis on how each student deals with homework, study and revision. However, it involves a lot more than this. It looks at every aspect of a student's life with the objective being to get the balance right between school-related work and everything else in their life. The information below is presented like a case study. It looks at how one student works her way through the year to try and achieve her goals. All of the important elements are covered at different stages in the book. The student in question is called 'Anne'. She availed of my One2One mentoring service from 2015 to 2017. She was looking to do Medicine at third-level so needed to achieve very high points. I worked with Anne through Fifth Year as well.

ANNE'S STORY

This is the story of her journey through Sixth Year (2016/2017) as seen through her involvement with One2One mentoring. I will tell her story through reports from the five meetings we had during Sixth Year.

Meeting 1 (Held at the start of Sixth Year)

The first meeting is very important. As much information as possible is gathered from the student. Key information would include how the student performed in Fifth Year, what commitments the student has for the coming year outside of school-related work, the strengths and weaknesses (academic and other) of the student, any concerns the student has in relation to the coming year, etc. Following is the report I prepared for Anne following **Meeting 1**.

Report on meeting with Anne on Saturday, 27 August 2016

Information from Anne at Meeting:

1. **Feedback on summer examinations at the end of Fifth Year:**

    Irish – Got 72%. Anne said that she could have done more by way of preparation.

    English – Got 82%. She had a time management issue. Chapter 7 is totally devoted to this.

    Maths – Got 75%. She was a little disappointed with this result. She wants to go over the returned script to see where she lost marks. She mentioned that she has really good notes from a course she did in a grind school last Easter.

    French – Got 69%. Anne found this a tough paper as it was Leaving Certificate Higher Level standard. She knows she is capable of a higher grade than this. She knows she has to work on comprehension and listening.

    Music – Got 82%. She said that she is going to get grinds to help with preparations for the practical. There was a comment on her Summer Report that she must work on the written side of things.

    Biology – Got 86%. She was really happy with this. She has total belief in her teacher here who motivates the class and works them hard.

    Chemistry – Got 57%. Anne admitted that she didn't prepare well for the exam. She focused more on other subjects so she knows she has ground to make up.

2. Anne has her heart set on Medicine at third-level. This requires around 550 points with a strong H-Pat. Her next choice would be

Psychology or Secondary School Teaching. Medicine, however, is what she really wants.

3. We reviewed Anne's targets for the Leaving Certificate. She had been doing Applied Maths in Fifth Year but has given it up.
   We set the following targeted grades:
   Irish (H3 – 77 pts)
   English (H1 – 100 pts)
   Maths (H2 – 88 pts [+ 25 bonus pts])
   French (H1 – 100 pts)
   Music (H1 – 100 pts)
   Biology (H1 – 100 pts)
   Chemistry (H2 – 88 pts).
   This would equate to **576 pts** + the bonus.

4. Anne said that she will be attending supervised study in school throughout the year. Mondays, Wednesdays and Fridays (3.30 p.m. to 7.00 p.m. with a 20-minute break); and Tuesdays and Thursdays (4.10 p.m. to 7.00 pm with a 20-minute break).

5. She said that she will be attending a talk in the Dublin Institute of Education on Medicine as a career with particular emphasis on the H-Pat.

6. Her main leisure activities for the year will be working out in the gym and socialising with friends.

7. Anne told me that she really enjoyed her trip to France during the summer. She was there for a month, attended classes every day, got great notes and a lot of experience of speaking French which will be great for the oral.

8. She also told me about time spent in the Gaeltacht during the summer. She was there for three weeks. She got great notes and had lots of experience of speaking Irish.

9. She said that she would consider Maths and Chemistry to be her 'weaker' subjects at the moment. A lot of work will need to be done in both.

10. Anne told me that they are doing examinations immediately after the October mid-term. She also said that the Mocks are taking place just before the February mid-term.

11. She said that she is prepared to apply herself to the plan we put in place and is dedicated to do everything she can to achieve her targeted grades.

Recommendations:

1.   The priority now is to plan the year really well. This involves drawing up **two work schedules** to start with: one for *normal school days* and one for *weekends*.

2.   On normal school days, Anne must do some extra school-related work on top of what she does at supervised study in school. On average, I am recommending a minimum of **four** hours *per day* over *seven days*.

   *   This will mean one **40-minute session** at home on Mondays, Wednesdays and Fridays.
   *   On Tuesdays and Thursdays, she will need to do **two 40-minute sessions**. Specific times should be set for these 40-minute sessions.

   It is important that Anne decides on days/times for her *workouts in the gym*. When everything is finalised, a specific time-table should be drawn up (see below).

3.   At weekends, I am recommending a minimum of **eight hours**. Anne is going to do all of this at home. I would like to see the main part of this done on Saturdays. She has no firm commitments at weekends in relation to leisure activities. Time will be fitted in for socialising with friends. I suggest six hours on Saturdays and two hours on Sundays. Again, a specific timetable should be drawn up (see below). All of this will bring real structure and consistency to her homework, study and revision.

4.   Anne worked hard through Fifth Year compiling her own **notes** in each subject. She should continue to do this when new material is covered in each subject. Also, she should work on developing her notes to the point where she has quality summarised notes for revision purposes for examinations. The objective is to eventually have a set of *short concise notes* in *every subject*.

5.   She should make sure to deal with **issues/problems/difficulties** as they arise. She should avoid putting them on the long finger. She must be decisive in relation to these. Find a way to sort them and do it. Once something is identified, a plan to sort it must be put in place and then commit to doing this as a matter of urgency. A number of issues were identified from the summer examinations at the end of Fifth Year (see Point 9, below). A way to deal with these must be found and implemented.

6.   Anne said that her two '**weaker**' subjects at the moment are Maths and Chemistry. Priority must be given to dealing with these without neglecting other subjects. I suggest that, when she has homework in these, do it first. And, when she is allocating time for study and revision, *make some time available for these.* This will help to bring them up to speed without neglecting the others. We will then review the situation at our next meeting before the October mid-term.

7.   She must monitor progress on an ongoing basis. Part of this involves looking closely at the quality of her work in school, at supervised study and at home. Look at the results in class tests and whether they are what they should be. Listen to comments from teachers and don't be afraid to take on board constructive criticism from those who know. Change anything that is not working.

8.   To gain maximum benefit from her time in **France** and at the **Gaeltacht** during the summer, she should compile her **own notes** from those she received.

9.   Summary of issues to be addressed from the summer exams at end of Fifth Year:
     *   **Catch-up work** to be done in Irish;
     *   **Time management** issue to be addressed in English;
     *   Make her **own set of notes** from those she got from Grind School in Maths;
     *   **Catch-up work** to be done on listening and comprehension in French;
     *   **Catch-up work** to be done on the written side in Music; and
     *   She knows that **work was neglected** in Chemistry at end of Fifth Year. This must be addressed.

Conclusion: Anne is in a very positive frame of mind about the year ahead. We have now put together a plan for the year. See work schedules below. She must now totally commit to these and focus totally on the process involved. The results will take care of themselves. At our next meeting, we will review everything, focus on making the work she does the best it can be, put a plan in place for the October mid-term and plan for the examinations she is doing after the break.

<u>Next Meeting</u>: Saturday, 22 October 2016

Work schedule for normal school days

Mondays	3.50 p.m. to 7.00 p.m.	Supervised study in school
	7.30 p.m. to 8.30 p.m.	Workout in gym
	9.20 p.m. to 10.00 p.m.	Session at home
Tuesdays	4.20 p.m. to 7.00 p.m.	Supervised study in school
	8 p.m. to 8.40 p.m.	Session 1 at home
	8.50 p.m. to 9.30 p.m.	Session 2 at home
Wednesdays	3.50 p.m. to 7.00 p.m.	Supervised study in school
	7.30 p.m. to 8.30 p.m.	Workout in gym
	9.20 p.m. to 10.00 p.m.	Session at home
Thursdays	4.20 p.m. to 7.00 p.m.	Supervised study in school
	8 p.m. to 8.40 p.m.	Session 1 at home
	8.50 p.m. to 9.30 p.m.	Session 2 at home
Fridays	3.50 p.m. to 7.00 p.m.	Supervised study in school
	7.30 p.m. to 8.30 p.m.	Workout in gym
	9.20 p.m. to 10.00 p.m.	Session at home

Work schedule for weekends

Saturdays	9.00 a.m. to 11.00 a.m.	Session 1 at home
	11.10 a.m. to 11.50 a.m.	Session 2
	12.00 p.m. to 12.40 p.m.	Session 3
	2.00 p.m. to 4.00 p.m.	Session 4
	4.10 p.m. to 4.50 p.m.	Session 5
Sundays	11.00 a.m. to 1.00 p.m.	Session at home

Sunday afternoons for socialising with friends.

Following the first meeting, Anne had a plan for the year with a work schedule for normal school days and one for weekends. We worked this out together. We fitted in her workouts in the gym and time for socialising with her friends. From my point of view, we included adequate time for all school-related work. The most important thing is that we now have real structure in place for the coming year. I firmly believe that this is essential if students are to achieve their targeted grades. It is particularly crucial for Anne as she is looking for very high points. It is now all about consistency through the year. We will review the situation at each meeting and assess how the plan is working.

I always break the year ahead up into periods. I then get each student to just focus on the period immediately ahead. I would break the year up in the following way:

Period 1:   from the start of the year up until October mid-term
Period 2:   the October mid-term
Period 3:   from October mid-term up until Christmas break
Period 4:   the Christmas break
Period 5:   the second term up until the February mid-term
Period 6:   the February mid-term itself
Period 7:   from February mid-term up until the Easter break
Period 8:   the Easter break itself
Period 9:   the last term up until when normal classes finish
Period 10: between the end of normal classes and the start of the Leaving Certificate examinations
Period 11: during the Leaving Certificate examinations

In relation to the targeted grades, I tell students to forget about these for the most part and to focus totally on the process involved in achieving them. Students need to focus on the period they are in and try to make everything they do the best it can be.

Every so often, I get them to take out their targeted grades and have a look at them. This can be good maybe on a night in the middle of winter when they might be finding the going tough. This is a gentle reminder about what it is all about. All this work is about giving them the opportunity to qualify for their chosen course at third-level which in turn leads in to the career of their dreams. It can give them a lift through the tough times. They then get back to their routine and focus on the process involved, a day at a time. We also review the targeted grades each time we meet to confirm we are on course to achieve them. These targets are not just what we hope to or would like to get. They are what we are *going* to get. We are going to make it happen. Nothing is going to come in our way. We must be that determined to succeed.

Meeting 2 (Just before the October mid-term)

This is a really important meeting. It is coming up to two months into Sixth Year. Each student should have settled into their routine at this stage. Any changes to the overall plan should have been made at this point. However, this is an ongoing process. Circumstances can change which means adjustments must be made to work schedules to reflect these. An important part of each meeting is reviewing how things have gone since the last meeting. Issues that were identified at the first meeting are looked at to see if satisfactory progress has been made. A big focus at this meeting is looking at the quality of work that is being done. Students are given a handout on key aspects for making work the best it can be. This is covered in Chapter 4 under the heading 'Doing Quality School-related Work at Home'. A plan is also put in place for the October mid-term break. It is very important to settle back into the normal routine once the break is over and this is emphasised. As the next meeting will not be until early January, a plan is put in place now for the Christmas break. Following is the report I prepared for Anne on our second meeting.

Report on meeting with Anne on Saturday, 22 October 2016

Information gathered from Anne at meeting:

1. **Review of each subject**

    Irish – Targeted grade for Leaving Certificate: H2 – 88 pts. Anne said that she feels a H2 might now be achievable. All aspects have been going well since we last met.

    English – Targeted grade for Leaving Certificate: H1 – 100 pts. She has been working on the time-management issues she spoke about last time. Making progress on this but still more to be done.

Maths – Targeted grade for Leaving Certificate: H2 – 88 + 25 pts. She did work on the returned script from the summer exams and addressed areas where she lost marks. She has also been working on the notes she got from the Grind School.

French – Targeted grade for Leaving Certificate: H1 – 100 pts. Anne said that she has been working on comprehension and listening which was an issue in the summer exams. She said that these are areas she struggles with so it will be an ongoing issue for her.

Music – Targeted grade for Leaving Certificate H1 – 100 pts. She said that her Mum and Dad have someone in mind for grinds on the practical side. She hopes this will start after the examinations in early November. She has been working on the written side but still struggling with some aspects. Her teacher has been absent for a while which hasn't helped.

Biology – Targeted grade for Leaving Certificate H1 – 100 pts. Everything continues to go well here. No issues at this point in time.

Chemistry – Targeted grade for the Leaving Certificate H2 – 88 pts. Anne is trying to do some catch-up work here. She admitted at our first meeting that she had neglected this subject a little at the end of Fifth Year. She is addressing this on a gradual basis. Progress is being made but more has to be done.

2. We reviewed the targeted grades and Anne is happy with what we have in place.

3. Medicine is still her top priority for third-level. It is her dream career. She is attending a talk on the H-Pat in the Institute of Education on 15 November.

4. Anne said that she has really settled into a good routine now. She is applying herself to the work schedules we put in place. She trusts them and is totally committed to them.

5. She said that she has not had too many **class tests**. She has performed well in those she has had. There have been two tests in Biology where she got 89% and 92%. She missed one in Music when she was out sick for a day. She had one in Chemistry covering three chapters and she got 77%. She has one coming up next week in English.

6. Her **grinds** in Maths are going well. She gets really good notes and she said that she does good follow-up work on these.

7. In relation to her **leisure** activities, her workouts in the gym have been a little bit hit-and-miss. Anne is going to address this and try to bring more structure to her workouts.

8. She said that she is trying to keep her **note-making** in all subjects up to speed but it can be difficult to always find the time.

9. In relation to the 'weaker' subjects we identified at the first meeting, Anne said that the grinds in Maths are really helping. Also, progress is good in Chemistry. As mentioned above, she scored well in a recent test. These remain her 'weaker' subjects moving forward.

10. Anne said that she is doing **questions from past papers** in some subjects. She is pleased with the standard of her answering in them.

11. As mentioned in my report on the first meeting, there are **examinations** in all subjects after the October mid-term. The exams will consist of 90-minute papers in all subjects.

Recommendations:

1. I am very happy with Anne's progress. She has settled into her routine really well. She has a positive approach to everything and has coped well so far. The important thing is not to look too far ahead and just to **focus on the immediate future**.

2. The overall plan Anne has in place is working really well so she should stick with it. She trusts the **work schedules** so she should commit to them moving forward.

3. My main concern at the moment has to do with Anne's leisure activities. Because she is such a diligent student, it is essential that she has **regular leisure/rest and recovery time**, etc. She needs to firm up on definite times for her workouts in the gym. Having structure here is just as important as having it for her school-related work.

4. I want Anne to keep a special **examinations notebook** for the examinations in early November. There are *three aspects* to this:
   a. Information about how preparations/revision go leading up to them.

b. Spending 10/15 minutes each evening writing up what didn't go so well in the exams that day.

c. Detailing where she lost marks when she goes through the returned scripts. Then, doing whatever follow-up work is necessary.

5. From now on, I want Anne to keep what I call a **'work in progress' notebook**. In this, she is to list important work which has to be done but she can't get to right now. Also, any difficulties/problems that need to be addressed but she can't get to yet. She should include areas in this which need to be addressed in each subject. She must check this regularly and prioritise what needs to be done. The idea is to tick off items as she addresses them.

6. Anne must have a specific **plan** in place for the **October mid-term break**. I am recommending school-related work on three days: Tuesday, Wednesday and Thursday. On each of these days, I want her to do eight hours' work.

There must be a timetable for each day, like below:

Session 1	8.30 a.m. to 10.30 a.m.
Session 2	10.45 a.m. to 11.45 a.m.
Session 3	12.00 p.m. to 1.00 p.m.
Session 4	1.30 p.m. to 3.30 p.m.
Session 5	3.45 p.m. to 4.45 p.m.
Session 6	5.00 p.m. to 6.00 p.m.

A big emphasis should be on **revision** for the **November examinations**. A special revision plan for this should be drawn up. This will then give Anne three days off at the start and 3 days off at the end. This is vital to have good rest and recovery time so that she is fresh and alert for the examinations immediately after the break and in good form for the period up to the Christmas break.

7. She must also have a specific **plan for the Christmas break**. I am recommending school-related work on six days, three days between Christmas and New Year with another three days between New Year and returning to school. On each of these days, I want her to do eight hours' work. There must be a timetable for

each day like what we had for the October mid-term (see Point 6, above).

Again, it is really important that Anne is careful at selecting the work she does. There should always be a good reason for doing work. It might be work prescribed from school, it might be adding to your notes, it might be doing some catch-up work from the areas listed in the 'work in progress' notebook, questions from past papers, revision for class tests coming up at start of the second term, follow-up work on the November exams, etc. It could also involve starting to revise for the Mock examinations.

8. **Summary of key aspects moving forward:**
   * **Trusting** her **work schedules** and **committing** to them.
   * Including **quality leisure/R&R time** in overall plan.
   * A **plan** for the **October mid-term.**
   * Use of **'work in progress' notebook.**
   * Use of **examinations notebook** for November exams.
   * A **plan** for the **Christmas break.**

Conclusion: The next few months are clearly mapped out for Anne. She has a really good routine in place for when normal school is on. Also, she has good plans in place for the October mid-term and the Christmas break. An important event coming up is the November exams. Anne must make sure to gain maximum benefit from these by applying herself to what we have in place. At our next meeting in early January, we will review everything, focus on exam technique and look to get the most out of the Mock examinations.

Next Meeting: Saturday, 7 January at 10.00 a.m.
   An important focus at the second meeting is making sure the quality of work is the best it can be at all times. I put a big emphasis on the work being done at home and in supervised study. I give them the following handout on how to make the work the best it can be. Again, I focus on the simple basics:

Doing Quality Work at Home and at Supervised Study in School

1. **Where will I do my school-related work?** You don't have to have a room to yourself. Just make where you do it the best it can be, free from distractions. Be consistent in relation to where you do your work. Don't be chopping and changing the location. At supervised study, select a spot away from friends/colleagues who may distract you.

2. **Mobile phones and electronic devices.** Leave them in another room during work sessions. At supervised study, turn them off. If you need to use a laptop for work purposes, you need to be very disciplined. Put it away once your work is completed.

3. **When do I do my school-related work?** This is where the **three work schedules** come in. Chapter 5 is devoted entirely to these. There is a specific timetable for normal school days, one for weekends and one for mid-terms/holidays, etc. You follow each schedule like you do with the timetable in school each day. This brings real structure to your work outside of class time. If any parts of the schedules are not working, change them. Find a better way. Once you have schedules in place that work for you, trust them and commit to them.

4. **Missed time.** When you miss a session, you owe this time back. It doesn't have to be done immediately. It must be done at some stage. Make a note of it in the 'work in progress' notebook and tick it off when you do it.

5. **Always do next day's homework first.** Homework has to be done so it makes sense to do it first. Take pride in doing your homework. Don't just do it for the sake of getting it done. Try to get the most out of it. You will achieve this by putting your all into it.

6. **Don't neglect weaker/less favoured subjects.** Prioritise doing work in these. When you have homework in these, do it first. When you are allocating time for study and revision, set aside time in these ahead of other subjects. However,

don't neglect other subjects either. This can all be achieved with good planning.

7. **Make your own short concise notes.** This should be done in every subject. In my opinion, it is the best type of work you can do. The process involved in compiling quality notes will lead to you retaining a lot of the material you cover. You will then have something very worthwhile to revise from at exam time. This is covered in more detail in Chapter 7.

8. **Always have a pen and paper to hand when studying.** Write down the main points of what you study or details of anything you don't understand. Then, have a plan to deal with them. Be determined to sort everything out.

9. **Always complete all scheduled work sessions.** This must happen even when you have no homework to do. This is what makes the difference. It might involve adding to your notes, working on something from the 'work in progress' notebook, revising for a class test coming up, working on something you had difficulty with in class, etc. There always should be a good reason for doing the work you choose.

10. **Plan revision carefully.** Revision must be undertaken in all areas on a regular basis. Then, test yourself on material revised by doing questions. Identify weak areas and have a plan to address them. Revisit areas on a regular basis. Make sure to keep on top of things. Don't leave it too long to go back over material. Good planning is essential here. Remember, 'practice makes perfect'.

11. **Identify difficult areas and have a plan to address them.** It might be as simple as doing an extra bit of work in a particular area. Sometimes, talking to one of your class colleagues can throw light on something you were having difficulty with. This is where it is good to have a small network of friends in each subject. You may be able to help them as well. It works both ways. In some cases, you may need to seek help from your subject teacher to sort out the difficulty. There is always a way. You must be determined to do whatever is necessary to overcome the difficulty.

12. **Spread your time across all subjects.** Don't neglect any subject. There can be a tendency to spend more time on

subjects you like or the subjects you are better at. This can sometimes happen without you noticing it. *Remember, your sixth counting subject for points, according to my theory, is your most important subject.* You must give each subject the respect it deserves.

13. **Have small breaks in between sessions at home.** Adequate rest and recovery is essential to make sure that the quality of work is the best it can be at all times. This becomes more important when you are doing school-related work late in the day. You need small breaks to recover and freshen up. You must get that second wind. The work you do at the end of the day must be of the same high quality as earlier in the day.

14. **Don't become complacent about your stronger subjects.** You should be determined to become even stronger at them. Don't take them for granted.

15. **The 'work in progress' notebook.** I have mentioned the significance of this already. When you don't have time to do something important immediately, enter details of it in this notebook. Check what you have listed in this notebook on a regular basis. Then, prioritise the items on the basis of how urgent they are. Tick off items when you address them. It will be an ongoing process.

Meeting 3 (Held at the beginning of January)

Every meeting is important but this one comes at the start of a really important period. The Mock examinations normally take place around the February mid-term break. They are a very important part of the overall preparation for the Leaving Certificate examinations. It is not all about the results in the Mocks but more about learning from the experience of doing them.

It is the students only opportunity for a full-scale practice for the real thing. In order to gain maximum benefit from doing them, a huge amount of effort must go into preparing for and performing at them. (There will be more information about that later.) This meeting comes at the start of the fifth period of the overall process. Period 5 takes us up to the start of the February mid-term break. For Anne, this includes the Mock examinations. Following is the report I prepared for her on our third meeting:

Report on Meeting with Anne on Saturday 7 January 2017

Information from Anne at meeting:

1. **Review of Subjects:**
    Irish – Targeted grade for the Leaving Certificate H2 – 88 pts. Anne mentioned that her teacher had retired. She really respected this teacher and was going to miss her. She got 67% in the November exams. Her preparations weren't great and she was disappointed with her essay. Also, she has done very little oral work to date.

    English – Targeted grade for the Leaving Certificate H1 – 100 pts. Anne said that she has been working hard on the time-management issues she has been having. She got 78% in the November exams. Time management was better but there was still work to be done. She also fell down on quotes in poetry.

    Maths – Targeted grade for Leaving Certificate H2 – 88 pts + 25 bonus pts. Still attending the sessions in the grind school. She got 58% in the November exam. Again, her preparations could have been better. Also, she messed up badly on the question on Financial Maths. She finds this section difficult.

    French – Targeted grade for Leaving Certificate H1 – 100 pts. She has always struggled a little with comprehension and listening. She continues to struggle despite a big effort to work on both. She is confident about the oral side following her time in France last summer. She got 75% in the November exam. Again, she lost marks in comprehension and listening.

    Music – Targeted grade for the Leaving Certificate H1 – 100 pts. Anne has started her grinds on the practical side. This is going well and it is boosting her confidence. She is still struggling with the theory side of things. She knows there is a lot of work to be done so she must get down to this. She was very disappointed with 63% in the November exam. It was mainly based on written work so there is more work to be done. She is focusing on singing for her practical. She sometimes neglects work in this subject and takes it a little for granted.

Biology – Targeted grade for Leaving Certificate H1 – 100 pts. Her teacher told them that they won't have covered all the course for the Mock examinations. She got 76% in the November exam. She really likes the subject and is happy with where she is with it. Again, her preparations could have been better for the November exam. Confident she can achieve her targeted grade.

Chemistry – Targeted grade for Leaving Certificate H2 – 88 pts. She is continuing to do catch-up work here. Anne had fallen behind in Fifth Year so gradually trying to catch up. More still to be done. Got 57% in November exam. However, class test results have been good since then and she has been scoring H2s. Confident she is on course to achieve this in the Leaving Certificate.

2.   Anne said that she was very sick over the Christmas break. It totally curtailed the amount of work she got done. The result was that she didn't get to do most of the prescribed work she was given along with other work she had planned to do.

3.   In relation to the H-Pat exam on Saturday, 25 February, Anne said that she has been getting a certain amount done in preparation. She got some early morning work done prior to Christmas as well as some at weekends. She is concerned that she is falling behind on what she should be doing. This will become more difficult now in the coming weeks when revision for the Mocks will be necessary.

4.   Her work schedules for normal school days and for weekends continued to go well.

5.   Anne said that she was getting to the gym on a regular basis before Christmas and that she finds these sessions really good. They complement her school work really well. She was unable to do workouts over the Christmas break because of her illness. She is hoping to get back to her normal routine from now on.

6.   She has completed all of her follow-up work on the November exams. She found the examinations notebook really helpful and using it made sure that she gained maximum benefit from doing them.

7.   She has been using the 'work in progress' notebook and finds it extremely useful. It is now a regular part of what she is doing and will be a very important aid in the months ahead.

Recommendations:

1. It was essential that Anne dealt with the impact of her illness over Christmas in a positive way. As I mentioned to her in an email over the Christmas break, the most important thing to do was to rest up so that a full recovery would happen as quickly as possible. Once this happened, all outstanding work could be done on a gradual basis. I recommended that she used her 'work in progress' notebook here. She needed to list all the important work that she didn't get to, prioritising and attending to it on an ongoing basis.

2. Anne must put a specific revision plan in place for the Mock examinations. She mentioned that they start on Monday, 6 February and run up to the February mid-term break. We are talking about a 4-week lead-in to the start of them. She should then have a specific revision plan for during them which will be linked to the exam timetable. It is very important that she uses the examinations notebook so that she can gain maximum benefit from doing them in order to perfect things for June.

3. A priority for Anne is the allocation of some time to prepare for the H-Pat exam which takes place on the second Saturday of the February mid-term break. This will take away somewhat from her preparations for the Mocks. This has to be done as the results in the H-Pat are an important part of the big picture. She can then allocate some time during the mid-term to do final preparations for the H-Pat.

4. On returning to school on Monday, Anne must settle into her normal routine which has worked really well for her so far. Total commitment to her work schedules is required. She must not overdo things by trying to get all the outstanding work done too quickly. This has to be gradual and she may have to suffer short term loss for long term gain.

5. Anne should study the two handouts I have given to her on 'Exam Technique' (see Chapter 7) and 'How to Gain Maximum Benefit from the Mock Examinations' (see below). She needs to tick all the boxes in relation to the points I have highlighted in these handouts.

6. She should have a definite plan in place for the February mid-term break. A big emphasis here will be on rest and recovery following

a hectic six weeks. Any work will be in relation to preparations for the H-Pat exam taking place on Saturday, 25 February.

7.   **Summary of key aspects moving forward:**
   * Do what is necessary to return to **full health** and maintain it.
   * Settle into **normal routine** from Monday onwards.
   * Draw up a **revision plan** for lead-in to **Mocks** and for during them.
   * Use **examinations notebook** for Mocks.
   * Use **'work in progress' notebook** for back log of work.
   * Have a realistic work **plan** for the **H-Pat exam.**

Conclusion: Anne has come through a tough time over the Christmas break. Her recent illness is only a temporary set-back. We said from the very beginning that she was going to achieve her targeted grades no matter what set-backs she has to face. She is still in a very strong position at this stage of her preparations for the Leaving Certificate. She must plan the next six weeks to incorporate all she is going to face – a revision plan for the H-Pat, a revision plan for the Mocks and doing the Mocks. A very busy period is coming up but a huge amount is to be gained from it. The most important thing about the Mocks is to learn all she can from the experience of doing them. This is where the examinations notebook comes in and the resulting follow-up work. It is her only opportunity for a full-scale practice so she must get everything out of it that she can. At our next meeting at the beginning of March, we will review everything with particular emphasis on the Mocks, look ahead to the remainder of the second term and put a plan in place for the Easter break.

Next Meeting: Saturday, 4 March at 10.00 a.m.
   A big emphasis in the above report is on exam technique and gaining maximum benefit from doing the Mock examinations. All aspects of good exam technique are dealt extensively in Chapter 7. Learning all you can from the experience of doing the Mocks is key to performing well in the Leaving Certificate. Below are some pointers from the handout I give to my students relating to this.

Gaining Maximum Benefit from the Mock Examinations

As mentioned above, the most important thing about the Mock examinations is to learn as much as you can from the experience of doing them. To help you to do this, you need to take the following points into consideration:

- Draw up a specific revision plan for the build up to the Mocks.
- Draw up another revision Plan for during the Mocks.
- Use an examinations notebook to record where things don't go to plan.
- Watch carefully how you manage time, both in relation to revising for the exams and performing during them.
- Do the necessary follow-up work from the information in the examinations notebook.
- Go through the returned scripts in detail. Make a note of where marks were lost on each paper. Do the necessary follow-up work to make sure the same marks won't be lost in June.
- Compare your results with your targeted grades. You don't have to be achieving your targets but results should indicate that you are on course to get them. Where you have fallen short, identify the reason why and make a plan to tackle it. Results will normally be better in the actual Leaving Certificate because you will have learned from the Mocks and you still have more than three months to go.
- Make a special note of anything that goes badly wrong in the Mocks. It might be something which came up that you hadn't a clue about or something that went totally wrong in your preparations.
- Don't be too down about poor result(s) in the Mocks. It is all about learning from such things. The Mock exams create opportunities to try things out. It is all about getting it right in June.

You can go on learning from the Mocks for a long time after they take place. You can space out the follow-up work so that it doesn't interfere with current work. This just requires good planning.

Meeting 4 (Held at the beginning of March)

A big emphasis at this meeting is feedback on the Mocks. The information in the examinations notebook and the notes on the returned scripts are vital here. I talk to each student about the follow-up work in each subject, how much has already been done and the plan for doing what still has to be done. The Mocks are not finished until the last bit of follow-up work is done.

I will check again at our last meeting at the beginning of May to see what the state of play is. There may be a number of issues that are only being addressed then. This doesn't matter as it can be a very drawn-out process. Once all the follow-up work is complete, each student should be in a really strong position to complete their preparations. Following is the report I prepared for Anne on our fourth meeting:

Report on meeting with Anne on 4 March 2017

Information from Anne at meeting:

1. **Review of Subjects:**
   Irish – Targeted grade for Leaving Certificate H2 – 88 pts. Anne said that her new teacher is really nice. She has been doing a lot of work on the oral. She has been practising with her brother and she finds this a great help. She got 87% in the Mock oral and a H3 overall. She ran out of time on Paper 2. She said that she didn't put the required level of work into her preparation for poetry. She knows she will for the Leaving Certificate. Happy overall with where she stands with Irish.

   English – Targeted grade H2 – 88 pts. Anne said that her preparations for the Mocks really suffered due to her illness over Christmas and the time she had to give preparing for the H-Pat. She got a H4 in the Mocks. Her teacher said that the correcting was not the best. She also said that Anne's writing was of a high standard for the most part. She said that it required a little more structure and more depth in places. Time management was fine which is encouraging as she has worked hard on this. Still work to be done on quotes in poetry.

   Maths – Targeted grade H2 – 88 + 25 pts. Got 46% in the Mocks. Anne said that she was unprepared. She had to leave some parts out. Her teacher was disappointed with her result as she knows she has real potential here. Anne has ongoing concerns which she plans to address. The sessions in the grind school will help here. Still struggling with Financial Maths.

French – Targeted grade H1 – 100 pts. She got a H3 in the Mocks. This didn't include a mark for the oral which she has yet to do. This should bring her up as she is strong here following time spent in France. Her teacher said that simple mistakes cost her. She still struggles a bit with listening and comprehension. Anne said that she is getting ongoing advice from her teacher on how to study certain aspects of the written paper.

Music – Targeted grade H1 – 100 pts. She got a H3 in the Mocks. Anne said she has been continuing with her grinds on the practical side. As mentioned at our last meeting, she is focusing on singing here. She feels she has neglected her work a little for the written paper. There is a lot of listening to music to be done. She said that she has done a certain amount but not enough. The practical exam will be done around the same time as the orals.

Biology – Targeted grade H2 – 88 pts. Anne got a H2 in the Mocks. She was really happy with this as she hadn't covered all she wanted to in her preparations. She had done a lot of work a while ago so was really pleased that she still retained what she covered back then. Happy overall with where she is.

Chemistry – Targeted grade H2 – 88 pts. She got a H4 in the Mocks. She knows there is still a lot of work to be done. It is a tough course with long answers expected to some questions. She said that she took a chance with some answers in the Mocks which didn't pay off.

2.	**Review of targeted grades for Leaving Certificate and comparison with results achieved in Mocks:**

Subject	Target Grade	Points	Mock Grade	Points
Irish	H2	88	H3	77
English	H2	88	H4	66
Maths	H2 (88 + 25)	113	H6 (46 + 25)	71
French	H1	100	H3	77

Music	H1	100	H3	77
Biology	H2	88	H2	88
Chemistry	H2	88	H4	66
Total		**577**		**456**

3. Anne said that she is fully recovered from the illness she suffered over Christmas and is now back to full health.

4. She said that she is happy with the way the H-Pat exam went. Anne added that she is really pleased that it is out of the way. It is difficult to predict the mark she will get as it was a hard exam. The results will be out around the time she will be sitting the written papers in the Leaving Certificate.

5. She said that she is happy with the work schedules we have in place for normal school days and for weekends. She is going to put a big emphasis on the 'weaker' areas in each subject in the coming weeks.

6. Anne said that her workouts in the gym have been going well since she got back to them following her illness. She finds them really good and she is able to take her mind away from all school-related matters.

7. She said that she is concerned about her performance in Maths in the Mocks. However, she was encouraged by her teacher's comments. She is going to put a big effort in over the coming weeks to get back on track to achieve a H2.

8. Anne said that she did use the examinations notebook during the Mocks and has been addressing the issues that arose. She is also working on the returned scripts in all subjects as she gets them back.

9. Her two 'weaker' subjects moving forward are Maths and Chemistry. She mentioned a plan for Maths above. She said that she will have a similar one in place for Chemistry.

Recommendations:

1. Anne was a little disappointed with some of her results in the Mocks. She is being too hard on herself. She must remember that her illness at Christmas set her back a lot. She has recovered well

from this and everything is back on track. Also, preparing for the H-Pat took a lot of her time and attention at a time when she would have been focusing totally on preparing for the Mocks. All in all, her **performance** at the Mocks was very creditable considering everything. As I have told her many times, the Mocks are all about learning from the experience of doing them. Once she has dealt with all of the issues listed in the examinations notebook and has completed all the follow-up work from the returned scripts, she will be in a really strong place moving forward to the Leaving Certificate itself.

2. I mentioned to Anne at the meeting that she must now have the **confidence and enthusiasm** for what lies ahead. A lot of progress has been made but a lot of work still has to be done. We are now approaching what I refer to as the 'business end' of things. She must be prepared to face all the challenges that lie ahead. She must be determined to succeed no matter what comes her way. She is in a strong position with three months to go to the start of the Leaving Certificate exams.

3. Anne must commit to her **work schedules** up to the start of the **Easter break**.

4. She must have a definite **plan** for the **Easter break** (see below).

5. There should be a big emphasis, from here on, on doing questions from **past papers** in all subjects. Every time she does a question, she should do follow-up work on any part she didn't perform well in. This will make sure that she will be stronger the next time she tackles a question like this. She must be very disciplined in relation to **time management** here.

6. A priority in the coming weeks will be preparing for the **Irish oral**, the **French oral** and the **Music practical**.

7. **Summary of important aspects moving forward:**
   * Being **confident and enthusiastic** about what lies ahead.
   * Tackling questions from **past papers** in all subjects and doing the necessary follow-up work.
   * Learning all she can from **class tests** and doing the necessary follow-up work.
   * Committing to her **work schedules** on a consistent basis up to the Easter break.
   * **Preparing** really well for the **orals** and Music **practical**.

* Prioritising work in **'weaker'** subjects, Maths and Chemistry without neglecting her other subjects.
* Completing her follow-up work on the **Mocks**.
* Making sure that she has the **balance** right between her school-related work and leisure/rest and recovery time. This becomes more and more important as we get closer to the Leaving Certificate. The regular workouts in the gym are essential for Anne.

Conclusion: Anne has come through a really tough period. She has done really well coping with everything she has had to face. Her immediate priority must be to make the next five weeks up to the Easter break the best it can be. When we meet next, we will review everything again and plan out the last three periods: the remainder of normal classes up to the graduation, from graduation until the Leaving Certificate begins and the period during the exams.

Next Meeting: Saturday, 22 April at 10 a.m.

A big emphasis in the above report is on the follow-up work from the Mocks. This is a critical part of preparing really well for the actual Leaving Certificate. With regard to planning ahead, having a definite plan in place for the **Easter break** is essential. I am recommending something like the following:

Easter Break Plan

* I am recommending eight days with school-related work and eight days of leisure/sport/family/rest and recovery for Sixth-Year students.
* I suggest they take the first Saturday and Sunday off.
* Then, do school-related work on Monday, Tuesday, Wednesday and Thursday of the first week. Do eight hours work on each of these days.
* Then, take Good Friday, Easter Saturday, Easter Sunday and Easter Monday off.

- Do school-related work on Tuesday, Wednesday, Thursday and Friday of the second week. Again, eight hours work on each of these days.
- Finally, take Saturday and Sunday off.
- On the work days, have a definite timetable.
- My suggestion for this is as follows:

Session 1	8.30 a.m. to 10.30 a.m.
Session 2	10.45 a.m. to 11.45 a.m.
Session 3	12.00 p.m. to 1.00 p.m.
Session 4	1.45 p.m. to 3.45 p.m.
Session 5	4.00 p.m. to 5.00 p.m.
Session 6	5.15p.m. to 6.15 p.m.

Again, it is really important to select the work you are going to do. It might include assigned work from school, questions from past papers, follow-up work from the Mocks, work listed in the 'work in progress' notebook, work on 'weaker' subjects or specific areas highlighted in individual reports. In Anne's case, it would be poetry in Irish and English, financial maths in Maths, listening and comprehension in French and listening in Music.

Each student should draw up their own plan and include individual elements such as grinds, special classes, etc. Include the kind of time I have in my recommendation which is **64 hours**. It is very important to have adequate rest and recovery time built in. Students must try to have a good balance as the last term will be very intense with the Leaving Certificate examinations at the end of it.

Meeting 5 (Held at the end of April/beginning of May)

It is really important to plan the remaining time well. At this point, I break the time remaining into **three periods** – *Period 9* (while normal classes remain), *Period 10* (from the graduation to the start of the Leaving Cert) and *Period 11* (during the exams). Special plans must be put in place for Periods 10 and 11. The regular work schedules are in place for Period 9. The following is the report I drew up on the fifth meeting with Anne.

Report on meeting with Anne on Saturday, 22 April 2017.

Information from Anne at meeting:

1. **Review of subjects:**

    Irish – Targeted grade for Leaving Certificate H2 – 88 pts). Anne said that her examiner was very positive about her performance in the oral. Anne herself was really pleased with the way she performed. She is confident about getting a top mark in it. In relation to preparing for the written paper, she has been focusing on doing essays recently. She is going to focus more on poetry and prose in the coming weeks. She knows what she has to do and is determined to do it.

    English – Targeted grade H2 – 88 pts. Anne said that she attended a really good course over Easter in the Art and Design College. She got really good notes to work on. She has been compiling her own notes from these. There was a big emphasis on how to get your points across. This is a concern of hers so it was really helpful. She is still concerned about certain aspects here but still working towards a H2.

    Maths – Targeted grade H2 – 88 + 25 pts. Anne said that she has been working really hard lately addressing her 'weaker' areas. She was recommended a website that specialises in questions from past papers. She found this helpful. She has been focusing on questions on calculus and financial maths. She is taking control of things herself now and is feeling more confident.

    French – Targeted grade H1 – 100 pts. Anne said that her oral went really well here too. She said that it lasted for sixteen minutes which is four minutes longer than the norm. Her teacher said it was a good sign. She got positive feedback from the examiner as well. In relation to the written paper, she has worked on questions on comprehension and is more confident now. She feels that the overall standard of her writing is improving. She knows she still has to work on listening.

    Music – Targeted grade H1 – 100 pts. She was happy with how the practical went. Anne said that it went better than the Mock practical. In relation to preparing for the written exam, she said that she is fine on the composing paper. She still needs to do more work on the listening paper. She still has notes to catch up on. She is still working towards a H1.

Biology – Targeted grade H2 – 88 pts. Anne is happy with the way things are shaping up here. She is wondering if it might be easier to get a H1 here than in Music. She knows exactly what she has to do and is determined to do it. On the down side, she knows that the marking can be hard in Biology which might come against her.

Chemistry – Targeted grade H2 – 88 pts). She is doing some catch up work here. There are still some chapters she has to work on. She knows that she then must link this with doing questions from past papers. In her head she is wondering will it be this or English that will count for points. (The importance of the sixth counting subject for points!)

2. Anne said that she has been applying herself to her work schedules. She has made some changes that improved her overall set-up. She is doing more at supervised study and less at home. The overall time is still the same. At weekends, she has been doing some of her work in the local public library.

3. She said that she has been doing less workouts in the gym. She has replaced it with walking and some jogging.

4. She said that she has continued doing follow-up work on the Mocks. She has identified areas that still need attention and she will continue the work here until all issues have been dealt with.

5. In relation to addressing her 'weaker' subjects, Anne said that she has been focusing more on Maths. The additional attention she is giving to Maths is having the desired effect with real progress being made. She is going to do the same with Chemistry in the coming weeks.

6. Anne has also identified that she needs more practice in doing questions from past papers in English. This is part of her plan for the coming weeks.

7. She said that she will be putting an increasing emphasis on doing questions from past papers in all subjects moving forward.

Recommendations:

1. I am breaking the remaining time up into three periods – Period 9 (for as long as normal classes remain), Period 10 (the two-and-a-half weeks up to the Friday before the start of the exams) and Period 11 (during the exams including the few days before they start).

2. A plan for Period 9 – Anne must apply herself to her regular work schedules for weekdays and weekends. She has made some changes in recent weeks involving more time at supervised study in school, less time at home and some time in the public library at weekends. She said that the overall total time is still the same. She should commit to this on a day-to-day basis and make the work she is doing the best it can be.

3. A plan for Period 10 – she mentioned that supervised study is available from 9.00 a.m. to 4.00 p.m. each day. She should then continue applying herself to her normal routine in the evenings and during the two weekends that remain. As supervised study will only be available during the day, she will have to do the evening sessions at home. The timeframe will still be the same.

4. A plan for Period 11 – this includes Saturday, 3 to Tuesday, 6 June. Any heavy detailed work should then be concluded by Monday, 5 June. Anne will then be in the final revision mode. She will have a special timetable for this which will be linked with the examinations timetable. The objective during this period is to be in peak form for the exams each day. As a result, revision the night before should be light enough so that Anne is fresh and full of energy the next day. This is where all the work put in over the last two years compiling her short concise notes really pays off. They are perfect as a source for the final revision work. Use should be made of any gaps in the exam timetable for revision purposes. Careful planning will make best use of this.

5. It becomes more and more important that the work you are going to do is planned really carefully for each session. Work must always be appropriate and she must make every session really count. Critical areas that spring to mind for me with Anne are: practice in answering certain questions in English, work on calculus and financial matters in Maths, acquire the notes she

needs on listening in Music and do the required work that still has to be done in Chemistry. There always has to be a good reason for doing the work she chooses.

6. The period we are facing into is going to be very demanding. It is essential that the overall plan incorporates adequate leisure/sport/family/rest and recovery time. This will be just as important as the work itself. The right balance must be found if the work is to reach the required standard at all times. Anne should build in the times when she goes for her walks/runs, meets her friends, etc. All of this requires very careful planning.

7. **Summary of key aspects for time remaining:**
   * Have the best **plans** in place for the three periods remaining and commit totally to them.
   * Get the most out of the remaining **classes**.
   * Big emphasis on doing questions from **past papers**.
   * Use the **'work in progress' notebook** for listing work to be done.
   * Focus totally on the **process** and not on the outcome (results).
   * Take it **one day at a time** and make the **work** you do the **best** it can be.
   * Identify any **difficulties/problems** and find a way to **deal with them**.
   * Be **decisive** in everything that you do.

Conclusion: Anne is in a really strong position now. She knows exactly what she has to do in the coming weeks to finish off the job. Careful planning of the three periods and a determination to commit to the plans she puts in place will get the job done. She then must believe in her ability and make it happen.

Note: Planning becomes even more important as the Leaving Certificate looms. And, of course, sticking to your plan. You have to adjust and adapt to what is going on. There can be a lot of distractions in the final run up to the start of the exams. Classes are beginning to wind down and the graduation takes place. The graduation is a very important occasion and should be enjoyed to the full. It should be included in the overall plan.

Anne made some small changes to her plan towards the end. She introduced some sessions in the local public library and did some walking/jogging instead of some gym sessions. However, there was very little change to her overall plan. There was a strong degree of consistency in everything that she did. There was very careful planning of each period and a total commitment to what she had in place. There was always a really good balance to everything and a total trust that what she had in place was the best for her at all times. This led to a total belief in her ability to succeed.

Anne got the points for Medicine and is now living her dream in her fifth year studying Medicine in Galway.

Testimonial from Anne

'During the two years leading up to my Leaving Certificate, I would have to say that the eight sessions (three in Fifth Year and five in Sixth Year) I spent with Tony were among the most important hours I put in in terms of my preparation. Tony's support, advice and kindness were invaluable to me. Tony helps each of his students in a very personal way. I was someone who came to Tony with a very ambitious goal that I was worried about not achieving. Tony took apart that goal, told me what I would need to get in each subject to achieve it and showed me where improvements needed to be made. In this way, he made my dream seem manageable and showed me that I was on track to achieving it. Tony showed me how to get the best out of every single thing I did in preparation for the Leaving Certificate and encouraged me to make time for the gym and seeing my friends. I was someone who spent a lot of time worrying that I wasn't doing enough and that I wasn't doing the right work. For me, the most valuable things Tony showed me were where I needed to spend my time and how to work in a smart and exam-focused way. Tony's experience and kindness made it easy to be honest about how to deal with problems I was facing. He is genuinely invested in getting his students to reach their full potential. I found that having someone so supportive and encouraging in my corner really motivated me to take everything he said on board in order to be the very best I could be.'

Chapter 3

From First Year to Sixth Year

It is extremely important that students settle into secondary school life as smoothly and quickly as possible. Most schools provide very good induction programmes for this. Summer camps take place in many schools as part of the induction process. In some cases, students make the transition with a number of their classmates from primary school which can make the process easier.

This may not be the case for a lot of students so the transition can be more traumatic. Notwithstanding the great support provided by the secondary school in question, each individual student requires a great amount of support and encouragement from parents and siblings at home. How they settle and perform in First Year can set the tone for the remainder of secondary school life. If they can form good habits early on, they will remain with them throughout secondary school and beyond.

I see the journey through secondary school as one with a gradual transfer of responsibility over to the student. First-Year students require a huge amount of hands-on support and encouragement. Initially, parents must watch very closely to see how their son or daughter is coping with the demands of secondary school life. Any obvious warning signs must be identified and dealt with. They will require help with certain aspects of their homework. Even where they are coping with it themselves, close parental supervision will be necessary. Gradually, they will begin to take more responsibility themselves. Parents will be able to stand back a little but close parental supervision will be necessary up to the end of the Junior Cycle.

It is very important that good habits are formed early on. Good structure will help even as early as in First Year. Specific work schedules should be in place right from the beginning of secondary school. I recommend that each First-Year student should spend 90 minutes per day at school-related work at home, Monday to Friday inclusive. This should be broken up into three 30-minute sessions. A special daily timetable should be in place for this. It shouldn't interfere with other activities, meal times, etc. It will then become part of their normal daily routine. It will be like the timetable they adhere to in school on a daily basis. They just accept that and apply themselves to it. The same will happen at home once they get used to it. I recommend something similar at weekends: six 30-minute sessions over the weekend. Again, a specific timetable in place that works around leisure/sport/family/ meeting up with friends/meal times, etc. Again, having a definite timetable in place brings the necessary structure.

For Second-Year students, I recommend two hours per day. This should be broken up into three 40-minute sessions. A special daily timetable should be in place for this. I recommend something similar at weekends. A total of four hours broken up into six 40-minute sessions.

For Third-Year students, I recommend three hours per day. This should be broken up into three 40-minute sessions and a one-hour session. A special timetable should be in place for this. I recommend something similar at weekends. A total of six hours broken up into two one-hour sessions and six 40-minute sessions.

For Fifth-Year students, I recommend the same as for Third-Year students. For Sixth-Year students, I recommend four hours a day. This should be broken up into two one-hour sessions and three 40-minute sessions. A special timetable should be in place for this. I recommend something similar at weekends. A total of eight hours broken up into four one-hour sessions and six 40-minute sessions.

It is not all about the amount of time each day, it is more about the structure and the quality of the work being done. Also, accommodating the leisure/sport/family/rest and recovery activities is an essential part of the overall plan. I also recommend a special plan in place for each of the four main breaks from school each year: October mid-term, Christmas, February mid-term and Easter. This will be discussed in more detail in Chapter 6.

> **Note:** The journey through secondary school requires a lot of hands-on support during the early stages with students taking on much more responsibility themselves as they approach the Leaving Certificate.

Attitude to School and All Matters Relating to It

A student's overall attitude to school and all matters relating to it is very important. If a student is totally negative about it, it is very difficult for them to be successful. I am not saying that a student must love going to school and be really enthusiastic about everything associated with it. We have to work really hard to create a positive attitude about it from an early stage.

Sometimes, this can be lost in the transition from primary to secondary school. Parents need to work very hard on this from the very start of secondary school. Students suddenly now have 9/10 teachers instead of one, are the smallest/youngest in the school, have totally new buildings/surroundings to get used to, new faces all around them in the classroom and a lot more changes to get accustomed to. New First-Year students can find all of this very daunting and can sometimes struggle to adapt. Their overall attitude to all of this plays a very important part in determining how they will get on.

Parents need to be very understanding about what they are going through and provide caring support at all times. This can be easier said than done at times as parents can have a number of children to be there for. For the most part, however, parents can take it for granted that students will be provided with the best of everything while they are at school. This is not nearly enough by itself, however. It is a proven fact that the most important influence on determining how a student succeeds through secondary school is what goes on in the home. There is no doubt that all parents want what's best for their children. Hence, the importance of being the best role models possible throughout their sons'/daughters' secondary school years.

> **Note:** Progress that is made in First Year can set the tone for what is to follow. Also, what goes on in the home has the biggest influence on how well a student performs through secondary school. Parents are the primary educators of their children.

Positive Approach to Doing School-related Work at Home

I see the journey through secondary school as one involving a gradual transference of responsibility from parents to students. During the early years of secondary school, a lot of hands-on involvement from parents is required. Throughout First Year, students will need a lot of assistance from parents when doing their school-related work at home. They will need direct help with their homework on a regular basis.

Even when they are able to do it themselves, parents must keep a close watch on how they are doing it. The emphasis should be on doing it as well as they can at all times. There is a danger that they get into the habit of just doing it to get it out of the way. Students can form bad habits early on in secondary school that will stay with them right the way through to the end of Sixth Year and beyond.

Parents have a very responsible role to play here in making sure that good habits are formed early on. A very important one is that they make sure that each student does the best work they can at all times. The attitude to doing homework is very important and must be developed as early as possible. Parents can contribute to children adopting a bad attitude to homework without really knowing it.

An example of this is a parent's attitude to getting homework done. Once they return home from school, a parent might immediately say 'get your books out and do your homework'. This is totally understandable as parents just want them to do it and may have other younger children to look after as part of a very busy routine.

I recommend that students are not forced to do homework immediately after they return home but that they have a specific schedule of work already arranged. Throughout the school day, they have to stick rigidly to a timetable. Once they have settled in each year, they become very comfortable with this and feel secure knowing what they have to face for the rest of the day. I am recommending that something similar happens at home. Such a schedule can work around the other important aspects of family life. Once they settle into such a routine, they will accept it and give their homework the respect it deserves. I look at this in more detail in Chapter 5 when looking at how to set up the best schedules of work for each individual student. Once this is done, it will help each student to develop a positive approach to doing homework, study and revision. This must happen very early on in secondary school before any bad habits set in.

> **Note:** First-Year students require close supervision when doing their school-related work at home. The need for this lessens as they form good habits. A definite routine for doing homework, study and revision at home is essential. A specific schedule must be in place to suit the needs of each individual.

Parents' Role in School-related Work Being Done at Home

As mentioned earlier, it is a well-known statistic that the home has the biggest influence on how students perform in school and all related activities. Parents want the best for their children at all times. Their role has a huge influence on their children's attitude to everything.

Parents are there for their children at all times and available to provide guidance and support when required. They are there to provide encouragement for their children in everything that they do. They need to be always available to listen and give their opinion on all issues raised. There is a great trust between parents and their children which works both ways. It is very important that children are totally open and honest with their parents also. This becomes more important as students make their way through the teenage years. Anything that concerns them should be made known to their parents no matter what age they are.

The home must always be the place where problems can be spoken about and solutions found. With regard to doing school-related work at home, I think that it is very important that as much structure as possible is brought to it. By this I mean that each student should have an individual schedule for doing their homework, study and revision that best suits their needs. There should be one of these for when they come home on normal school days, one for weekends and one for mid-term breaks and holidays. I go into all of this in much more detail in Chapter 5.

> **Note**: Students must be totally open and honest with their parents about all issues they are concerned about.

Doing Quality Work at All Times

All students must be encouraged to do the **best work** they can at all times. Sometimes, students just want to get the work done and out of the way. This is understandable but not the best practice. It is all about the quality of what you do rather than how quickly you get it done. Habits can be formed very early on in relation to this. First-Year students must be encouraged to present their work to **acceptable standards** at all times. The adults around them should complement them on work well done and bring their attention to work that is below acceptable standards. They must be encouraged to take pride in the work they do at all times.

Eventually, each student can become their hardest critic. Before a student reaches this point, parents must assume this role. Parents must be honest with their children when assessing their work. If a student has clearly done their best, one cannot be critical of their efforts. They may need help in a particular area which must be provided. Where work is careless, attention must be drawn to it as improvements can be made with increased efforts.

Students must be conscious of the importance of doing the best work they can. This will have been emphasised to them throughout their years in primary school. It becomes a whole new ball game in secondary school when they have to answer to many teachers not just one. The supervision by parents in this regard early in First Year will ensure that good habits are formed which will remain with students forever. There will be a full section on 'doing quality work' at a later stage.

> **Note**: It is all about each student doing the best they can in everything they are involved in. They must aim for a consistency across the board in every aspect of their lives. Below standard performance in one area can very easily spill over into other areas.

Setting Targets

Short-term targets

I am referring here to everything a student is involved in on a daily basis. The objective each day should be to do your very best in everything you are involved in. This is easy in relation to the things you like doing and are good at. It becomes more difficult when it comes to doing things you don't like as much or that you are not as good at.

We should start each day determined to do our best with every task or challenge we are faced with. With things that are going really well, we must make sure that this continues on a consistent basis. We must not take anything for granted. If we become complacent in any way about a specific area or task, we will not maintain the high standards we had achieved up to that point.

If something does not go well despite our best efforts, we must be more determined than ever to get it right the next time. We must be aware of not applying ourself as well as we should later each day. As we become more tired as the day progresses, it requires a greater effort to make sure that the required standards are maintained at all times. We must make sure that we take sufficient breaks to allow our bodies to recover from all the exertions earlier in the day.

We should not be discouraged by things not going well. We cannot be expected to perform at the top of our ability all the time. We are going to have bad days when things don't go our way. We must do everything we can to make sure that this does not happen on a regular basis. When things go wrong, we must learn from this and make sure that we do not repeat the same mistakes. Sometimes, we have to go wrong to eventually get it right. We should not make the same mistake twice. When students get into the right frame of mind early on in First Year in relation to doing their best, this will remain with them throughout secondary school and beyond.

> **Note:** Effective performance is all about taking care of the little things and the bigger picture will take care of itself.

Medium-term targets

I am referring here to everything encountered along the way to achieving long-term targets. The long-term targets are those we set ourselves to achieve in the end-of-year examinations. For Sixth-Year students, it's the Leaving Certificate examinations. The medium-term ones would include ongoing class tests, progress reports from teachers, end-of-term examinations and other such progress reports/feedbacks.

Obviously, we want to do as well as we can in all of these but this is not the main objective. It is all about practising and learning from the experiences gained so that we can perform at our best in the end-of-year examination. We should not be looking too far ahead. First-Year students should not look beyond the examinations they face in June. Third-Year students should not look beyond the Junior Certificate examinations. Sixth-Year students should not look beyond the Leaving Certificate examinations. Everything in the lead up to the end-of-year examinations should be geared towards peaking at these. Medium-term targets are all about learning from the experiences along the way, testing ourselves on a regular basis and becoming stronger as a result of all we go through during the year. It is all about putting ourselves in the strongest possible position for the main examination.

> **Note:** Plan, prepare and test yourself along the way so that you are in the strongest possible condition to achieve your long-term targets.

Long-term targets

I am referring here to the grades you are going to get in the examinations at the end of the year. They are not the grades you hope to get or would like to get. It needs to be more definite than this. Because of this, a lot of thought must go into arriving at these grades. You must be capable of achieving them but they must stretch you at the same time. Once you arrive at them, you must know that you will be very proud of them once they are achieved. You should write them down and refer to them on a regular basis. These are what all the hard work is for. If you are having a particularly bad day, you should have a look at them to remind you what all the hard work is for. You should also review them from time to time and make changes where necessary.

You should not make a change just to make life easier for yourself. You might find that you have become stronger in a certain subject and now are confident that you can achieve a higher grade. In such circumstances, you should change to a higher grade to reflect the improvement you have made. Conversely, if you begin to struggle in a certain subject despite your best efforts, you should change to a lower grade to reflect the difficulty you are experiencing in this subject.

Targeted grades must be realistic and obtainable at all times. Because of this, it is essential that we re-appraise the situation from time to time to make sure that the targeted grades are what they should be. To be able to do this accurately, we must monitor progress on an ongoing basis to make sure that we are on schedule to achieve the targeted grades and realise our potential. We will look at this under a separate heading called 'Monitoring Progress' in Chapter 8.

> **Note:** You must always have something to aim for. Targeted grades in your next big examination fits the bill here. Achieving these is what will drive you on when the going gets tough.

Chapter 4

Reality Check

Every student should assess where they are starting from before a new school year commences. This is vital at the beginning of First Year. The student will need the help of their parents when doing this at the start of secondary school life and this has to be a really honest appraisal of the student's position. This requires an analysis of each students' strengths and weaknesses. If a student has any special needs requirements, this must be highlighted and appropriate help sought. Their new secondary school must be made aware of the circumstances so that the best plan can be put in place.

Strengths must be listed. This list can include subjects/subject areas or aspects of the students' general make-up. The priority with strengths is that they must continue to be strong in these areas and we must not take them for granted in any way. In fact, we must be determined to become even stronger if that is possible.

With regard to weaknesses, the first thing is to identify them. The next stage is to put a plan in place to address them. We should not accept that we are always going to be weak in a particular subject area or that a weakness is just a specific part of our make-up that we cannot change. I am not saying that we can become brilliant at everything but we can certainly get better with the right attitude. We must identify why we are weak in an area and look at ways that we can improve. There are always ways we can improve if we have the right attitude and the determination to do what is required. These self-assessments should take place on a regular basis throughout secondary school. The start of each year is an appropriate time to do them.

In Leaving and Junior Certificate years, it is a good idea to assess the situation a few times during that year. It is very important that we don't continue with something that is not working. A better way must be found and put in place. If a student is having difficulty in a particular area, a way of dealing with it must be found. It normally does not take very much to find solutions in such cases. We sometimes can let such situations drift on which can lead to a worsening scenario. What started off as being a small issue can develop into a much more serious situation. We must be decisive and take action when required.

It is usually easy to solve problems if we identify them early, find a solution and put it in place. Parents have a real hands-on role to play in this during the early years in the Junior Cycle. Students will then take more responsibility themselves as they enter into the Senior Cycle. They will identify areas of concern and recommend ways of dealing with them.

> **Note:** Regular reality checks must take place on an ongoing basis to assess how we are doing. Early recognition of a problematic area is essential before too much damage is done.

School-related Work at Home

Students follow a strict timetable during school hours. Everything is organised for them in a very efficient manner. They know exactly what they have to face each day. I recommend that they bring the same kind of structure to their school-related work at home.

For this to happen, each student should draw up a timetable that suits their individual needs. I recommend that they have three schedules: one for normal school days, one for weekends and one for mid-terms/holidays, etc. A lot of thought must go into drawing up these schedules. It is very important to get the right balance between school-related work and their leisure/sport/family activities. Later on, we look at how to draw up these schedules making sure that all the student's activities, both school-related and non-school-related, are catered for. With regard to the school-related work, one of the top priorities is to make sure that the quality of the work is the best it can be at all times.

Doing Quality School-related Work at Home

There are many influences that affect the quality of the school-related work that is done at home. Below we will look at some of these.

Where do I do my school-related work?

You must try to make where you do your work the best it can be. You do not have to have a separate room all to yourself. It is what you make of the location that matters. You must make it as comfortable as possible and free from distractions that you have control over. An example of this would be your mobile phone. Don't have it in the room with you. Where there are distractions that you cannot control, you must have tunnel vision to eliminate them from your mind.

You must keep your workspace as tidy as possible at all times. Make sure you know where everything is so that you can put your hands on anything you need. This requires you to be organised at all times. This comes easy to some students and less easy to others. It is something you have to work on. Try to be as organised as you possibly can. I do not accept it when certain students say that they can never be organised. We can all become more organised if we have the mindset to do this. We don't have to have everything perfectly in its place at all times. What we need is reasonable order which will lend itself to quality work being done.

> **Note:** You must make your work space at home the best it can be. You must make it possible for yourself to do the best work you can at all times.

When do I do my school-related work at home?

This depends on individual circumstances in the home. A special schedule must be drawn up for it. This will depend on the demands in the home. This should be worked out at the beginning of each school year.

For students in the Junior Cycle, parents should sit down with their son/daughter to plan this. You are working it out together rather than forcing them to do it. It has to be flexible as it may have to change due to changing circumstances. The starting point is listing the commitments the parent will have on an ongoing basis. The schedule will have to work around these. Also, you must list the commitments the student will have outside of their school-related work. Again, the schedule will have to work around these. Once all of this has been established, you can look at drawing up a schedule of work for normal school days.

Parents should avoid forcing their son/daughter to get down to their homework immediately after they come in from school. This sends out the wrong message to them. I can understand why parents can adopt this approach as they want to get students to do their homework as soon as possible. It is one less problem we have to deal with later in the day. However, what this does is create an attitude of 'get homework done and out of the way'. Remember, they have had a long tough day in school and they may not be in the right frame of mind for doing 'quality work' as soon as they arrive home. When a definite schedule is in place they know when they will be doing it each day, which can be comforting to them. It becomes like the timetable in school which they are very used to. I recommend a break when they come in from school which will put them in the right frame of mind for doing their school-related work.

How long should I spend on homework?

The next thing we need to sort out is how long they need to spend on homework each day. This will depend on the amount of homework they get. I recommend that **First-Year students** spend **one-and-a-half hours** at their school-related work each normal school day.

They should always have enough time to complete their homework and have some time left over for some study and revision. Some days, they may just have enough time to complete their homework. They may even have to put in a little extra time to complete it. On other days, they may only have a little homework and will be able to do more study and revision. No matter what, they must always complete the one-and-a-half hours. This discipline will set them up really well for when they have to take more responsibility themselves later on.

Once the best schedule is in place and they have settled into it, it will work really well. It is always difficult working out how long they should spend at it each day. There is no one answer to this. As we know, it is all about what they do during the time rather than how long they spend on it. Always having some time for additional work over the time spent at homework is the key. This is what makes the difference as far as I am concerned. Otherwise, there is an attitude of getting homework done and out of the way. It takes some time and effort to get the best set-up in place. But once this is achieved, real progress can be made.

> **Note:** Having a specific schedule for students at home, like their timetable in school, really works. Even though they won't admit it, children and young people like having real structure in their lives. They get security from knowing exactly where they stand and what they have to do.

Deciding on what to do

This is very straightforward in relation to homework. Students need to just follow the instructions given. They will require a lot of help and support from parents in the early stages of secondary school. Students should be encouraged to work on their own initiative as much as possible. Parents should keep an eye on what they are doing at all times. Parents should not end up doing some of their work for them. Parents can make things too easy at times. It is a matter of getting a good balance here. Parents need to try and get students to work things out for themselves as much as possible.

When students are really struggling, then parents need to step in and provide help and support. And parents must provide direction at all times. Early on, parents can help out a lot with regard to suggestions on what to do once homework is complete.

The more practice you get in all aspects of your work, the stronger you will become. It might be simply doing similar questions to the ones you had for homework. Parents should encourage students to do work in subjects you might be a little weaker at or might not like as much as others. You need to keep an eye on things to make sure you are not neglecting any subject.

Parents must be able to identify any warning signs that might appear suggesting that a son/daughter is losing interest in a particular subject. If identified early, something like this can normally be sorted out very easily. If not attended to, the situation will become worse and worse leading to a total dislike for the subject in question or an inability to make satisfactory progress in it.

Students must spread themselves across all subjects as best they can. Watch out for subjects where homework is not allocated on a regular basis. It may be necessary to allocate study/revision time to these when possible. Outside of homework, thought must go into what is going to be done in the remaining time. Having decided on this, the quality of the work must always be the best it can be. Parents should do their best to oversee this during the early stages of secondary school until students can gradually take responsibility themselves.

> **Note:** Students should choose carefully when deciding on what to do when they have time available for study and revision. It might be that you have a test coming up and need to revise for it. It might be that there was something you were struggling with in class and you need to do some extra work on it. It might be that you have a project to complete and the deadline is fast approaching. There are always lots of good reasons for doing additional school-related work!

Don't neglect weaker/less favoured subjects

It is always easy to work on favourite subjects. There is a natural tendency to do this. In the same way, we can leave work on weaker/less favoured subjects until the end. As time goes on, the gap between the favourite subjects and the weaker/less favoured subjects can widen. We must prioritise work on the weaker/less favoured subjects in order to address the problem.

These subjects should be identified and a plan devised to deal with the situation. I always suggest that students do homework in these subjects first. When there is time for study/revision, work in these subjects should take priority. A simple change in attitude like this can make a big difference. At times we can convince ourselves that we don't like something or that we are not good at it. If this attitude continues, the situation will only get worse. What was only a small issue can quickly develop into a serious problem. We might end up totally disliking a subject or having absolutely no confidence in our ability to succeed in it. This need not happen if we address the situation early enough.

I am not saying that we can all be brilliant at everything. With determination and a good plan, we can all improve even in subjects we think we are weak in and may not like as much as others. It is all about becoming the best we can be in all subjects. This might mean excelling in certain subjects and becoming competent in others.

We may need help in a subject we are struggling in. It may not be enough to do more work in it yourself. This should be the first stage in dealing with the situation. If you are still struggling despite putting in a lot of additional effort yourself, you may require outside help. This can come in the form of grinds. Grinds can be great if used for the right reasons. Grinds should never replace the class work in that subject, however. It should be just an additional help to deal with a specific difficulty. The primary source of support should always be from your subject teachers backed up with your work. Remember, a weaker/less-favoured subject may end up being your most important one. My 'sixth counting one for points' concept highlights this. It could be the one that brings you over the line in relation to the points required for your preferred choice of course at third-level.

Note: Be determined to improve in subjects you are weaker at or may not like very much. Don't become negative about a situation like this, instead be committed to getting better.

Making use of weekends

There is a huge amount of time from when we finish in school on Friday evenings to when we return on Monday mornings. If we plan our weekends carefully, we can facilitate all the things we want to do and still make time for the required amount of school-related work.

It is very important that every student gets involved in quality leisure activities. Weekends provide the ideal opportunity to pursue these. With good planning, all activities (within reason) can be accommodated. We will address this in detail in Chapter 5 when we are looking at planning weekend sessions.

I recommend that students in all years of secondary school do a certain amount of school-related work at the weekend. The amount of time a First-Year student spends on school-related matters should be relatively small. As they progress through secondary school, the time spent will increase.

When they reach Sixth Year, there should be a sizeable amount of time allocated to school-related work at weekends. At this stage, it is still possible to accommodate everything with good planning. Getting First-Year students into the habit of doing a certain amount of school work at weekends is essential.

It is very important that they get used to this right at the beginning of their secondary school lives. Involve them in the planning process for this. Make them see that they won't have to give up anything to be able to do it. Once the plan is in place, they know what they have to face each weekend. After a few weeks, it will become part of their routine. They will gain comfort from knowing exactly what they have to do each weekend. The fact that it only takes up a small amount of time available throughout the whole weekend will seem very reasonable to them.

Once students accept that they must do a certain amount of school-related work at weekends at the beginning of First Year, the amount of time can be increased as they move from year to year. Weekends are an ideal opportunity to do some additional work. Once homework is complete, the remainder of the time can be spent on study and revision. Time can be spent making your own notes (see more on this in Chapter 7). Work can be done in preparation for class tests that are coming up. Work can be done on something you found difficult in class during the week. A lot of thought must go into deciding on what you are going to work on. There should be a good reason for selecting something to work on. Students will need a lot of help from parents in this regard during their early years in secondary school. Gradually, they will be able to make decisions for themselves and will be capable of becoming more responsible for their own actions.

Weekend schedules should be flexible to a certain degree. If circumstances change, you must be able to adjust the schedule accordingly. Leisure and family activities are very important and must be catered for. Work schedules are not fixed in stone and can be adjusted to facilitate changes in other activities. Where a set-up is working really well, changes should only be made for very good reasons.

> **Note:** Weekends provide a great opportunity to get additional work done by way of study and revision.

Making use of mid-term/holiday periods

There are four main holidays to look at: the October mid-term, the Christmas break, the February mid-term and the Easter break. These breaks from school are a great opportunity to re-charge the batteries following an intense period of school activity. With this in mind, I normally recommend students take the weekend at the beginning of a mid-term off and do no school-related work at all. They have earned this and need a complete break. I also recommend them to take the second weekend off as well as they must make sure to be fresh and rested when returning to school following the mid-term.

I recommend that any school-related work should be done on the days in the middle of the break. A schedule should be drawn up by each student in advance of the start of each mid-term. The Christmas break is a little more complex because of the way the dates can fall. I always recommend that students take a good break around Christmas itself and then another one around New Year. They can then plan their work schedule around this.

The Easter break is a little like Christmas in that I also recommend that students take a good break over the Easter weekend. It is always more straightforward than Christmas in that it always includes two full weeks. Like with mid-terms, I usually recommend that they take the weekend at the beginning and the weekend at the end off for the same reasons given for mid-term breaks. Samples of schedules for different year groups are provided later in the book to indicate what we are trying to achieve.

> **Note:** Breaks are a great opportunity to get some quality work done but students must make sure to include a lot of quality leisure time as well. As always, it is about getting the balance right.

The importance of sport/leisure/extra-curricular/family activities

The saying 'all work and no play' is very appropriate here. It is very important that students get the balance right between school-related matters and other things in their lives. An over-emphasis on school-related matters will not work in the long term.

When we are involved in school-related matters, be it in school or at home, we must give our total commitment to it. When we are away from it, we must be able to shut it out of our minds. If we are unable to do this, it is a strong indication that something is wrong. We must identify why this is happening and find a way of dealing with it. Focus and concentration play a key role here. When we are in class or doing school-related work at home, we must be able to shut everything else out of our minds. To do this, we must have tunnel vision.

In the same way, when we are engaged in our leisure activities, we should not be concerned about school-related matters. Involvement in sporting activities is great for this. The fact that most sporting activity takes place out in the fresh air is really good for us. It is a great way of clearing our minds of all matters academic.

The competitive element of sport is also very good for us. It is very important that we are competitive in our school-related work as well. We must want to be the best we can possibly be in all matters pertaining to school. We can get this competitive edge from our involvement in sport and other extra-curricular activities. We can also learn how to be a good team player which will also benefit us greatly in our school lives. If we are not into sport, it is essential that we have other interests outside of school-related work. These interests can be in the school or elsewhere.

The crucial thing is that we have interests outside of the academic side that can take our minds off the issues and pressures there. Such involvements show us how to take responsibility and teach us leadership qualities which are vital for success in our school work and in examinations. In order that school-related matters and leisure/extra-curricular activities work well together, good planning must take place to facilitate both.

Note: Involvement in strong leisure/extra-curricular activities will improve the quality of school-related work providing that a good plan is in place to incorporate both.

Chapter 5

The Three Schedules of Work

A top-class service is provided for us while we are attending school. To supplement this, we must make sure that we have the best plan in place outside of school to cope with all school work and other important things in our lives. Everything is organised for us really well in school. The service provided is second to none. It is vital that we use the time at our disposal outside of school in the best way possible. To do this, I recommend that we have three schedules of work: one for normal school days, one for weekends and one for mid-term breaks and holidays.

Schedule 1: Normal School Days

I am recommending that a specific schedule is drawn up for this. We are talking about weekdays when students have attended school each day. The first things that must go into this schedule are the student's commitments outside of their school-related work.

I am often asked the question 'How long should they spend at their homework, study and revision?' There is no correct answer to this. My normal reply to this is that it is more about the quality of the work rather than the amount of time spent at it. When pressed to give a more specific answer, I say that they should include enough time to complete homework for the next day along with some time for study/

revision. There might be something urgent that needs to be addressed but is not part of formal homework. When pressed about the minimum amount of time that should be spent, I recommend **one-and-a-half hours for First-Year students, two hours for Second-Year students, three hours for Third-Year students, the same for Fifth-Year students** and **four hours for Sixth-Year students.**

The **schedule** should be put together at the beginning of the year. It may take a few weeks to get it right as changes may need to be made to make it work. Once it is the best it can be and it facilitates all the requirements of that individual student, it should not be changed except under exceptional circumstances.

One important rule is that **all sessions must be completed irrespective of the homework situation.** If there is no homework to be done on a particular day, the sessions timetabled for that day must still be completed. This is what will make the difference. Situations like this provide an ideal opportunity to get quality study/revision done.

Also, **sessions missed are owed back.** The time lost must be made up at some stage. I also recommend that students don't commence their school-related work immediately on returning from school. They have just completed a tough day at school so need some time to recover and freshen up. I advise that there should be a small break following each session, particularly towards the end of each day. Exceptions can be made to this where a student is in the middle of something and does not want to break the momentum. A session may be extended to accommodate this.

There must be a **minimum of disruption to the family because of the timetable.** Meal times should not be disrupted as a result of the timetable. The objective is to bring as much structure as possible to school-related work at home similar to what they experience in school.

Supervised study in school should be included in these schedules. Once the student gets used to it, they will become very secure with the set-up that is in place. Students love to know what the boundaries are. Following are three examples of the type of schedules I recommend be in place – one for a First-Year student, one for a Third-Year student and one for a Sixth-Year student.

Example 1: The First-Year Student

Seán is in First Year. He plays on the school rugby team. He has training on Tuesday and Thursday afternoons from 4.00 p.m.–5.00 p.m. On these days, he returns home from school at 5.30 p.m. He has matches on Wednesday afternoons and is home at 5.00 p.m. He attends scouts on Friday evenings from 7.00 p.m.–9.00 p.m. On Mondays and Fridays, he returns home from school at 4.00 p.m. He was weak at Irish through primary school. His parents have arranged grinds for him to get him up to speed. This takes place at home from 7.00 p.m.–8.00 p.m. on Mondays. He also plays for a soccer club with matches/training taking place on Saturday mornings between 10.00 a.m. and 1.00 p.m. He attends scouts on Sundays which normally takes up most of the morning. The following is my recommended schedule for Seán for normal school days.

Mondays	
Session 1	4.30 p.m. to 5.00 p.m.
Session 2	5.10 p.m. to 5.40 p.m.
Session 3 (Irish grind)	7.00 p.m. to 8.00 p.m.
Tuesdays	
Rugby training	4.00 p.m. to 5.00 p.m.
Session 1	7.00 p.m. to 7.30 p.m.
Session 2	7.40 p.m. to 8.10 p.m.
Session 3	8.20 p.m. to 8.50 p.m.
Wednesdays	
Rugby Match	2.00 p.m. to 5.00 p.m.
Session 1	7.00 p.m. to 7.30 p.m.
Session 2	7.40 p.m. to 8.10 p.m.
Session 3	8.20 p.m. to 8.50 p.m.
Thursdays	
Rugby Training	4.00 p.m. to 5.00 p.m.
Session 1	7.00 p.m. to 7.30 p.m.

Session 2	7.40 p.m. to 8.10 p.m.
Session 3	8.20 p.m. to 8.50 p.m.
Fridays	
Session 1	4.30 p.m. to 5.00 p.m.
Session 2	5.10 p.m. to 5.40 p.m.
Scouts	7.00 p.m. to 9.00 p.m.

Note: The big emphasis for First-Year students is on the student settling into secondary school life. You should not be expected to do a lot of school-related work at home. It is more about you getting used to a routine for doing your work. You should be involved in the planning of this routine at the beginning of the year. You need to feel like you are part of the decision-making process that leads to the drawing up of the above schedule. It is important that other activities actually appear on the schedule. You will see it as an overall plan rather than one just to do with school-related work. After a short while, you will accept it as part of your daily routine just like the school timetable.

Parents must keep a close watch on the quality of the work students are producing in these sessions. It will eventually lead to them taking more pride in their work. Parents should then be able to stand back a little as their son/daughter takes more responsibility themselves. It may be necessary to make small changes to the schedule over the first few weeks. It is really important that the best plan is in place to suit the needs of each student. The difficult part is getting it up and running. After a short while, the student will become used to it. They will accept it like they do the timetable at school. They will see that they have plenty of time for other things as well like being involved in rugby and Scouts in Seán's case. Students become aware early on that they have to complete each session on the schedule irrespective of homework. It gets them used to doing some study and revision early on. That it is not just about homework. It is all about good structure and settling into a good routine. Once the final schedule is arrived at, a copy should be on view where the student does their work and, also, one for the parents. In time, the student will gain comfort from the structure that is in place. The hour at the grind is included in the overall time (seven-and-a half-hours) for the five days.

Example 2: The Third-Year Student

Susan is in Third Year. She plays on the school hockey team. They have training on Tuesday afternoons from 4.00 p.m. to 5.00 p.m. and play matches on Wednesday afternoons (2.00 p.m. to 4.30 p.m.) and Saturday mornings (10.00 a.m. to 12.30 pm). She also attends drama on Friday evenings (7.00 p.m. to 8.30 p.m.) and on Sunday mornings (11.00 a.m. to 12.30 p.m.). She was struggling with Maths towards the end of Second Year. She has grinds on Monday afternoons (5.00 p.m. to 6.00 p.m.). She is taking Music as an examination subject. She has an extra lesson on piano on Thursdays (4.00 p.m. to 5.00 p.m.). The following is my recommended schedule.

Mondays	
Maths grind	5.00 p.m. to 6.00 p.m.
Session 1	7.00 p.m. to 7.40 p.m.
Session 2	7.50 p.m. to 8.30 p.m.
Session 3	8.40 p.m. to 9.20 p.m.
Tuesdays	
Hockey training	4.00 p.m. to 5.00 p.m.
Session 1	7.00 p.m. to 8.00 p.m.
Session 2	8.10 p.m. to 8.50 pm
Session 3	9.00 p.m. to 9.40 p.m.
Wednesdays	
Hockey match	2.00 p.m. to 4.00 p.m.
Session 1	5.00 p.m. to 6.00 p.m.
Session 2	7.00 p.m. to 7.40 p.m.
Session 3	7.50 p.m. to 8.30 p.m.
Session 4	8.40 p.m. to 9.20 p.m.

Thursdays	
Piano lesson	4.00 p.m. to 5.00 p.m.
Session 1	5.15 p.m. to 5.55 p.m.
Session 2	7.00 p.m. to 8.00 p.m.
Session 3	8.10 p.m. to 8.50 p.m.
Session 4	9.00 p.m. to 9.40 p.m.
Fridays	
Session 1	4.15 p.m. to 5.15 p.m.
Session 2	5.25 p.m. to 6.05 p.m.
Drama class	7.00 p.m. to 8.30 p.m.
Session 3	9.00 p.m. to 9.40 p.m.

Note: With the Junior Certificate examination at the end of the year, the main emphasis is on preparing for that. The main objective is to put the student in the strongest position to perform to their ability at these examinations. I am recommending a minimum of three hours of school-related work on weekdays outside of class work. In Susan's case, it is a bit less on Tuesdays and Fridays which is fine. Her total for the five days is thirteen hours and 40 minutes (1 hour and twenty minutes less than the recommended fifteen hours). This should be enough to cover homework and some study/revision under normal circumstances.

The Mock examinations during the second term are a very important part of the preparations for the Junior Certificate examinations. We look at how to gain maximum benefit from this exercise at a later stage. Students must be prepared to slot in a few additional sessions at key points in the year. The lead-in to the Mocks would be one such occasion. Students should review how their schedule is working on a regular basis. From time to time, they should grade their performance in sessions. If they are targeting a top grade in a particular subject, the quality of their work should be of the highest standard on a consistent basis. It is really important that Third-Year students settle into their routine as quickly as possible with the Junior Certificate examination at the end of the academic year. The structure in place will make sure that school-related work will be consistent throughout the year.

Example 3: The Sixth-Year Student

Andrew is a Sixth-Year student. He has very definite views on the path he wants to take at third level. The course he wants to gain entry to requires in excess of 500 points. He is a member of the senior rugby squad and has to make a serious commitment to this. He has training sessions on Mondays and Thursdays after school, which finish at 5.30 p.m. He has matches on Wednesday afternoons. He attends early supervised study in school on Tuesdays and Fridays from 4.00 p.m. to 6.00 p.m. He has two grinds on Saturdays. The Maths grind is from 12 noon to 1.00 p.m. and the one in English is 3.00 p.m. to 4.00 pm. Both of these are at home. My recommended schedule is as follows.

Mondays	
Rugby training	4.00 p.m. to 5.30 p.m.
Session 1	7.00 p.m. to 8.00 p.m.
Session 2	8.10 p.m. to 8.50 p.m.
Session 3	9.00 p.m. to 9.40 p.m.
Session 4	9.50 p.m. to 10.30 p.m.
Tuesdays	
Supervised study	4.00 p.m. to 6.00 p.m.
Session 1	7.00 p.m. to 7.40 p.m.
Session 2	7.50 p.m. to 8.30 p.m.
Session 3	8.40 p.m. to 9.20 p.m.
Wednesdays	
Rugby Match	2.00 p.m. to 4.30 p.m.
Session 1	5.00 p.m. to 6.00 p.m.
Session 2	7.00 p.m. to 8.00 p.m.
Session 3	8.10 p.m. to 8.50 p.m.

Session 4	9.00 p.m. to 9.40 p.m.
Session 5	9.50 p.m. to 10.30 p.m.
Thursdays	
Rugby Training	4.00 p.m. to 5.30 p.m.
Session 1	7.00 p.m. to 8.00 p.m.
Session 2	8.10 p.m. to 9.10 p.m.
Session 3	9.20 p.m. to 9.50 p.m.
Session 4	10.00 p.m. to 10.40 p.m.
Fridays	
Supervised study	4.00 p.m. to 6.00 p.m.
Session 1	7.00 p.m. to 7.40 p.m.
Session 2	7.50 p.m. to 8.30 p.m.
Session 3	8.40 p.m. to 9.20 p.m.

Note: Ideally, for Sixth-Year students, we are looking for a minimum of four hours on weekdays for homework, study and revision. For Andrew, because of his commitment to rugby, it is just not possible to achieve all of this. We are short just two hours (eighteen instead of the recommended twenty hours), which is fine. Andrew may have to look at making some of it up at a later stage.

Also, I would recommend that he has a work plan available for rugby days in case the training session/match does not take place. Once the rugby season is over, a new schedule should be drawn up to make use of the additional time that would become available. It would be a mistake to have absolutely no physical activity as he has been so used to it. I would recommend some gym sessions to replace some of the time that was taken up with rugby. It would be good to include some running/jogging as well. If possible, some team sport as well to replace the rugby matches. A group from the rugby squad could get together to arrange some tag rugby or five-a-side soccer a few times a week.

While rugby continues, Andrew must make sure that he has sufficient time in his schedule to complete homework with most of the study/revision taking place at weekends. It may be necessary to slot in a few early morning sessions before school starts. Andrew's objective is to achieve in excess of 500 points so that he can gain entry into his chosen course. His scheduling during the year should prepare him to achieve this.

Schedule 2: Weekends

There is a huge amount of time between the time a student leaves school on Friday afternoon and returning on Monday morning. It is an ideal opportunity to get some additional school-related work done. Like with the schedule for normal school days, the first things to go into the schedule for weekends are the leisure/sport/family activities. Once this is done, we can then put our sessions for school-related work in.

The main focus at weekends should be on study and revision. The objective on Fridays is to complete homework that has to be done for Monday. If there is still outstanding homework to be completed, it should be done in the early sessions of the weekend. The sessions should be planned carefully around all the other activities. We must get the balance right between providing adequate time for rest and recovery while fitting in the required number of sessions for quality work to be done.

Again, the question normally asked is in relation to how much time should be allocated to school-related work at weekends. As mentioned before, it is more about the quality of the work rather than the amount of time spent at it. I normally recommend a minimum of twice what is recommended for normal school days. For First-Year students, this would be a total three hours, for Third-Year students, a total of six hours and for Sixth-Year students, a total of eight hours.

Also, any shortfall in time spent during the week should be made up at weekends. Where possible, I like to avoid allocating work to be done on Sunday evenings in order that the student can rest and relax in preparation for returning to school afresh on Monday morning. It may not always be possible to achieve this, particularly for senior-level students because of the volume of work that has to be accommodated.

What one should always avoid is leaving homework that has to be done until the last moment on Sunday evening. Students can do without this pressure. Also, rushing things at the last moment does not lead to quality work.

Example 1: The First-Year Student

Seán is in First Year. Remembering that he plays for a soccer club on Saturday mornings from 10.00 a.m. to 1.00 p.m. and is involved with the scouts on Sundays all morning, my recommended schedule is as follows:

Saturdays	
Soccer match/training	10.00 a.m. to 1.00 p.m.
Session 1	2.00 p.m. to 2.30 p.m.
Session 2	2.40 p.m. to 3.10 p.m.
Session 3	3.20 p.m. to 3.40 p.m.
Sundays	
Scouts	9.00 a.m. to 1.00 p.m.
Session 1	2.00 p.m. to 2.30 p.m.
Session 2	2.40 p.m. to 3.10 p.m.
Session 3	3.20 p.m. to 3.50 p.m.

Note: The above sessions are reasonably flexible. If a change needs to be made to facilitate a family activity or something similar, this can be done. Where possible, the sessions should take place as per the schedule. We may need to try things out at the beginning of the year in order to eventually arrive at the best set-up for all concerned.

It is extremely important that First-Year students become used to this discipline as early as possible. They will get used to the schedule after a few weeks and will feel good about knowing the amount of time they will be spending at school-related work each weekend. It will look good to them as it is only a very small part of all the time that is available each weekend.

The above is just the minimum amount of time recommended. It may be necessary to add a little more time as the year progresses. I would suggest that a few sessions are added in the lead up to the Christmas examinations and again for the summer examinations. This will help them get used to having to do a little more at key moments in the year.

The most important thing about work at weekends is that, for the most part, it is additional work over and above homework that has to be done. This helps with deciding on how much time should be spent on school work. They should not just think of school-related work at home just being homework. It should be more than this. The earlier they appreciate this, the better. It is all about First-Year students realising that they must set aside some time at weekends for school-related work.

Example 2: Susan, the Third-Year Student

Remembering that she has hockey matches on Saturday mornings and drama on Sunday mornings, my recommended schedule is as follows:

Saturdays	
Hockey Match	10.00 a.m. to 1.00 p.m.
Session 1	2.00 p.m. to 3.00 p.m.
Session 2	3.10 p.m. to 3.50 p.m.
Session 3	4.00 p.m. to 4.40 p.m.
Session 4	4.50 p.m. to 5.30 p.m.
Sundays	
Session 1	9.30 a.m. to 10.30 a.m.
Drama	11.00 a.m. to 12.30 p.m.
Session 2	2.00 p.m. to 2.40 p.m.
Session 3	2.50 p.m. to 3.30 p.m.
Session 4	3.40 p.m. to 4.20 p.m.

Note: We are looking at a minimum of six hours school-related work over the weekend for a Third-Year student. Again, the emphasis is on balance. There should be plenty of time for recreation with work sessions built around this. The schedule arrived at should lead to the best school-related work being done. Most of the work being done at the weekend should be study and revision. This will depend on all homework being done already. If some of the time spent at weekends is on homework, additional sessions will have to be added to facilitate this. If the two sessions allocated on Friday are not sufficient to complete homework, additional session(s) will have to be added at weekends for this. It will take a bit of playing around with it at the beginning of the year to arrive at the best schedule. The weekend situation may have to change on a week-to-week basis depending on the level of homework given.

Where possible, students should apply themselves to the schedules that are in place. Where this can't happen, students must come up with an alternative plan for that day. The same amount of time must be included in the temporary plan. The following weekend, they revert to the original plan.

Example 3: Andrew, the Sixth-Year Student

Remembering that he has Maths and English grinds on Saturdays. My recommend schedule is as follows:

Saturdays	
Session 1	9.00 to 10.00 a.m.
Session 2	10.10 a.m. to 11.10 a.m.
Maths grind	12.00 p.m. to 1.00 p.m.
Session 3	2.00 p.m. to 3.00 p.m.
English grind	3.00 p.m. to 4.00 p.m.

Sundays	
Session 1	9.30 a.m. to 10.30 a.m.
Session 2	10.40 a.m. to 11.40 a.m.
Session 3	11.50 a.m. to 12.50 p.m.

> **Note:** The minimum recommended time for school-related work at weekends for a Sixth-Year student is eight hours. The time spent at the two grinds is included in this. This means finding time for six one-hour sessions.

The objective for a Sixth-Year student aiming for very high points is making every session the best it can be. Choosing what to do in each study/revision session assumes greater importance. Making the work done in each session the best it can be is a priority. I recommend that students grade themselves on the work they do in certain selected sessions.

Take a session in English as an example and say that student has targeted a H1 in the Leaving Certificate. The quality of work must be of H1 standard consistently in study sessions if they are to be on course to achieve that. Additional sessions will need to be included at weekends to meet demands for certain circumstances, for example in the lead-up to Mocks or in preparation for orals, etc. I am including one-hour sessions here to make it possible for students to fit more work into each session.

Schedule 3: Mid-terms/Holiday Periods

What's being referred to here are the October mid-term, the Christmas break, the February mid-term and the Easter break. These are ideal opportunities to get additional work done. It is just as important to use them to re-charge the batteries and gain some much-needed rest and recovery. As mentioned before, it is all about balance between the school-related work and the leisure/extra-curricular/family time.

What work is done during these periods depends on the individual circumstances in question. It might be a good time to catch up on a subject or part of a subject that has been neglected a little. It might be to do some work on a subject area that was causing difficulty. It might be to use it as an opportunity to get up to speed with note-making in a certain subject. There may be tests coming up that must be prepared for. It might be a project you have to complete as the deadline for submitting it is approaching. You might need to do some preparatory work for the orals. There are always good reasons for doing additional work. A lot of thought must go into planning these opportunities so that maximum benefit can be derived. We should draw up a list of urgent matters that need to be addressed and prioritise them in order of importance. The 'work in progress' notebook can be used here. See more on this in Chapter 9. We have already looked at how to make best use of mid-terms/holiday periods.

October mid-term break

To get the balance right, the week must be planned carefully in advance. Again, it is about bringing as much structure to the situation as possible. Any commitments for the week must be taken into consideration. As a general rule, out of the nine days in the break, I recommend six days off with only three days to include school-related work. This gives students a really good break following a demanding start to the school year and, at the same time, gives them the chance to get quality work done.

Example 1: Seán, the First-Year Student

Seán is going on a trip with his soccer club over the first weekend including the Monday. He is away all of the following Friday on a camp with the scouts. The following is my recommended schedule:

Saturday, Sunday and Monday	
Trip with soccer club	
Tuesday	
Session 1	9.30 a.m. to 10.00 a.m.
Session 2	10.10 a.m. to 10.40 a.m.
Session 3	10.50 a.m. to 11.20 a.m.

Wednesday	
Session 1	10.00 a.m. to 10.30 a.m.
Session 2	10.40 a.m. to 11.10 a.m.
Session 3	11.20 a.m. to 11.50 a.m.
Thursday	
Session 1	2.30 p.m. to 3.00 p.m.
Session 2	3.10 p.m. to 3.40 p.m.
Session 3	3.50 p.m. to 4.20 p.m.
Friday	
Scouts	
Saturday and Sunday	
Rest/leisure/family time	

Note: I have included a slightly later start on Wednesday to give Seán a little more time to have a lie in. The sessions on Thursday are in the afternoon because he has arranged to meet up with a group of friends in the morning. Again, the emphasis for the First-Year student is on just a little school-related work during the October mid-term. I am recommending four-and-a-half hours broken up into nine 30-minute periods.

I always recommend, where possible, that the student takes both weekends off, irrespective of what year they are in. In this case, Seán is away for the first weekend so it happens automatically. I suggest the second weekend off because they need a good break before returning to school for the remainder of the first term. If they have been prescribed any homework, this must be done ahead of any other work. They could then focus on work on their weaker subjects with direction on this from their parents.

Example 2: Susan, the Third-Year Student

She is attending classes in Irish and English in a grind school each weekday morning from 10.00 a.m. to 11 a.m. She is involved in an Irish dancing Feis on Saturday and Sunday at the end of the break. The following is my recommended schedule:

Saturday and Sunday	
Rest/leisure/family time	
Monday	
Grind School	10.00 a.m. to 11.00 am
Free time for rest of day	
Tuesday	
Grind school	10.00 a.m. to 11.00 a.m.
Session 1	2.00 p.m. to 2.40 p.m.
Session 2	2.50 p.m. to 3.30 p.m.
Session 3	3.40 p.m. to 4.20 p.m.
Wednesday	
Grind school	10.00 a.m. to 11.00 a.m.
Session 1	12.00 p.m. to 1 p.m.
Session 2	7.00 p.m. to 7.40 p.m.
Session 3	7.50 p.m. to 8.30 p.m.
Session 4	8.40 p.m. to 9.20 p.m.
Thursday	
Grind school	10.00 a.m. to 11.00 a.m.
Session 1	2.00 p.m. to 3 p.m.
Session 2	3.10 p.m. to 3.50 p.m.
Session 3	4.00 p.m. to 4.40 p.m.
Session 4	4.50 p.m. to 5.30 p.m.
Friday	
Free day	
Saturday and Sunday	
Irish dancing Feis (all day both days)	

Note: I am recommending a minimum of twelve hours in total over the break for Third-Year students. As much as possible, I want it done on the three middle days of the break (Tuesday, Wednesday and Thursday). The time spent at the grind school is to be included in the twelve hours. Susan has arranged an afternoon out with her friends on Wednesday so the sessions are in the evening. Any work prescribed from the school should be done first. Time should be allocated for work on areas of concern. Questions should be done from past papers.

Example 3: Andrew, the Sixth-Year Student

He is a member of the senior rugby squad. He has training on Tuesday and Thursday afternoon from 3.00 p.m. to 5.00 p.m. He has a weights session in the gym on Wednesday morning from 10.30 a.m. to 12 noon. He has Maths grind on Monday evening from 7.00 p.m. to 8.00 p.m. and an English one on Friday afternoon from 4.00 p.m. to 5.00 p.m. The following is my recommended schedule:

Saturday and Sunday	
Leisure/sport/rest activities	
Monday	
Maths grind	7.00 p.m. to 8.00 p.m.
Otherwise free.	
Tuesday	
Session 1	9.00 a.m. to 11.00 a.m.
Session 2	11.10 a.m. to 12.10 p.m.
Session 3	12.20 p.m. to 1.20 p.m.
Rugby Training	3.00 p.m. to 5.00 p.m.
Session 4	7.00 p.m. to 8.00 p.m.

Wednesday	
Session 1	9.00 a.m. to 10.00 a.m.
Workout in gym	10.30 a.m. to 12.00 p.m.
Session 2	2.00 p.m. to 4.00 p.m.
Session 3	4.10 p.m. to 5.10 p.m.
Session 4	7.00 p.m. to 8.00 p.m.
Thursday	
Session 1	9.00 a.m. to 11.00 a.m.
Session 2	11.10 a.m. to 12.10 p.m.
Session 3	12.20 p.m. to 1.20 p.m.
Rugby training	3.00 p.m. to 5.00 p.m.
Session 4	7.00 p.m. to 8.00 p.m.
Friday	
English grind	4.00 p.m. to 5.00 p.m.
Otherwise free	
Saturday and Sunday	
Leisure/sport/rest activities	

Note: I am looking for a minimum of eighteen hours of school-related work to be done over the break. Again, if possible, I would like most of it to be done during the three middle days. This will create a lot of opportunity for leisure/rest time. The two hours spent at the grinds are included in the eighteen hours. I have included a few two-hour sessions which gives Andrew the opportunity to work on his time management. He could select a few questions from past papers that should take two hours in total and test himself on this. Again, a big emphasis should be on selecting the work to be done. As I have mentioned before, there always should be a good reason for doing the work you choose. This requires good planning.

Christmas break

Normally this break lasts a little over two weeks. There is a big focus on the Christmas period and the New Year period. I like students to have good time off around both of these periods to enjoy the festivities. Good planning is required to achieve this. Again, we look to bring structure to the time allocated to school-related work so that plenty of time is freed up to enjoy Christmas and the New Year. The details below are based on the school calendar for Christmas/New Year of 2017/2018.

Example 1: Seán, the First-Year Student

The only commitment Seán has over the holiday period, on top of the normal festivities, is a day of activities with the Scouts on Wednesday, 3 January. The following is my recommended schedule:

Saturday, 23 December; Christmas Eve; Christmas Day and St Stephen's Day are all free to enjoy the Christmas festivities.	
Wednesday, 27 December	
Session 1	10.00 a.m. to 10.30 a.m.
Session 2	10.40 a.m. to 11.10 a.m.
Session 3	11.20 a.m. to 11.50 a.m.
Thursday, 28 December	
Session 1	3.00 p.m. to 3.30 p.m.
Session 2	3.40 p.m. to 4.10 p.m.
Session 3	4.20 p.m. to 4.50 p.m.
Friday, 29 December	
Session 1	10.00 a.m. to 10.30 a.m.
Session 2	10.40 a.m. to 11.10 a.m.
Session 3	11.20 a.m. to 11.50 a.m.
Saturday, 30 December; New Year's Eve and New Year's Day are all free to enjoy the New Year festivities.	

Tuesday, 2 January	
Session 1	10.00 a.m. to 10.30 am
Session 2	10.40 a.m. to 11.10 a.m.
Session 3	11.20 a.m. to 11.50 a.m.
Wednesday, 3 January	
Day of activities with the Scouts	
Thursday, 4 January	
Session 1	3.00 p.m. to 3.30 p.m.
Session 2	3.40 p.m. to 4.10 p.m.
Session 3	4.20 p.m. to 4.50 p.m.
Friday 5, January	
Session 1	7.00 p.m. to 7.30 p.m.
Session 2	7.40 p.m. to 8.10 p.m.
Session 3	8.20 p.m. to 8.50 p.m.
Saturday, 6 and Sunday, 7 January	
All free for family/leisure/sport/rest activities	

Note: Looking for nine hours in total here: eighteen 30-minute sessions. I have put three sessions in the afternoon spread across two days as Seán has arranged to meet up with friends on those mornings. This is another example of how we work around other commitments made by students. This is a priority when planning work schedules.

Example 2: Susan, the Third-Year Student

She is attending classes in a grind school on the mornings of Thursday 4 and Friday 5 January, from 9.30 a.m. to 12.30 p.m. Also, she is involved in Irish dancing for the whole day on Friday, 29 December. The following is my recommended schedule:

Saturday, 23 December; Christmas Eve; Christmas Day and St Stephen's Day all free to enjoy the Christmas festivities.

Wednesday, 27 December

Session 1	9.30 a.m. to 10.30 a.m.
Session 2	10.40 a.m. to 11.20 a.m.
Session 3	11.30 a.m. to 12.10 p.m.
Session 4	12.20 p.m. to 1.00 p.m.

Thursday, 28 December

Session 1	2.30 p.m. to 3.30 p.m.
Session 2	3.40 p.m. to 4.20 p.m.
Session 3	4.30 p.m. to 5.10 p.m.
Session 4	5.20 p.m. to 6.00 p.m.

Friday, 29 December

Irish dancing	

Saturday 30, December; New Year's Eve; New Year's Day and Tuesday, 2 January are all free to enjoy the New Year festivities.

Wednesday, 3 January

Session 1	9.30 a.m. to 10.30 a.m.
Session 2	10.40 a.m. to 11.20 a.m.
Session 3	11.30 a.m. to 12.10 p.m.
Session 4	12.20 a.m. to 1.00 p.m.

Thursday, 4 January

Dublin School of Grinds	9.30 a.m. to 12.30 p.m.
Session 1	2.30 p.m. to 3.30 p.m.
Session 2	3.40 p.m. to 4.20 p.m.
Session 3	4.30 p.m. to 5.10 p.m.
Session 4	5.20 p.m. to 6.00 p.m.

Friday, 5 January

Grind School	9.30 a.m. to 12.30 p.m.
Session 1	2.30 p.m. to 3.30 p.m.

Session 2	3.40 p.m. to 4.20 p.m.
Session 3	4.30 p.m. to 5.10 p.m.
Session 4	5.20 p.m. to 6.10 p.m.
Saturday, 6 and Sunday, 7 January	
Free for leisure/sport/rest/family time	

> **Note:** For Junior Certificate students, I am looking for 24 hours over the holiday period. We settled for 21 hours here, which is fine. The time Susan spends at the Grind School is to be included in this. We then have twenty sessions over five days. This means that all school-related work is done on five days thus leaving a huge amount of time for leisure/rest and recovery, etc.

Example 3: Andrew, the Sixth-Year Student

He has rugby training on Tuesday, 2 January and Thursday, 4 January from 2.00 p.m. to 4.00 p.m. He has a gym session on Wednesday, 3 January 9.30 a.m. to 10.30 a.m. He has a Maths grind on Friday, 29 December from 5.00 p.m. to 6.00 p.m. and an English one on Friday, 5 January from 7.00 p.m. to 8.00 p.m. The following is my recommended schedule:

Saturday, 23; Christmas Eve; Christmas Day and St Stephen's Day are all free to enjoy the Christmas festivities.	
Wednesday, 27 December	
Session 1	9.00 a.m. to 11.00 a.m.
Session 2	11.10 a.m. to 12.10 p.m.
Session 3	2.00 p.m. to 4.00 p.m.
Session 4	4.10 p.m. to 5.10 p.m.
Thursday, 28 December	
Session 1	2.00 p.m. to 4.00 p.m.

Session 2	4.10 p.m. to 5.10 p.m.
Session 3	7.00 p.m. to 9.00 p.m.
Session 4	9.10 p.m. to 10.10 p.m.
Friday, 29 December	
Session 1	9.00 a.m. to 11.00 a.m.
Session 2	11.10 a.m. to 12.10 p.m.
Session 3	2.00 p.m. to 4.00 p.m.
Maths grind	5.00 p.m. to 6.00 p.m.
Saturday, 30 December; New Year's Eve and New Year's Day are all free to enjoy the New Year festivities.	
Tuesday, 2 January	
Session 1	9.00 a.m. to 11.00 a.m.
Session 2	11.10 a.m. to 12.10 p.m.
Session 3	12.20 p.m. to 1.20 p.m.
Rugby training	2.00 p.m. to 4.00 p.m.
Session 4	5.00 p.m. to 6.00 p.m.
Session 5	7.00 p.m. to 8.00 p.m.
Wednesday, 3 January	
Gym session	9.00 a.m. to 10.30 a.m.
Session 1	11.00 a.m. to 1.00 p.m.
Session 2	2.00 p.m. to 4.00 p.m.
Session 3	4.10 p.m. to 5.10 p.m.
Session 4	5.20 p.m. to 6.20 p.m.
Thursday, 4 January	
Session 1	9.00 a.m. to 11.00 a.m.
Session 2	11.10 a.m. to 12.10 p.m.
Rugby training	2.00 p.m. to 4.00 p.m.
Session 3	4.30 p.m. to 5.30 p.m.
Friday, 5 January; Saturday, 6 January and Sunday, 7 January – free for leisure/sport/rest time	

Note: I look for 36 hours of school-related work from Sixth-Year students over the Christmas break. We settled for 34 hours here, which is fine. I try to fit it into five/six days so that they have a lot of free time as well. Again, work to do should be chosen very carefully. With the Mock examinations looming in February, students have to focus on preparing for them. The Christmas break is a good time to put a plan in place. If you are to gain maximum benefit from doing the Mocks, you must put a lot into preparing for them. The time Andrew spends at grinds is part of the 34 hours.

February mid-term break

This is similar to the October mid-term in that it is exactly the same length. For First-Year students, I recommend exactly the same work schedule for this break. For Junior and Leaving Certificate students, it depends on when the Mocks are. For the purpose of the two examples here, they do the Mock examinations immediately before the break. I have found that this is the case in most schools. One student I am working with this year did some papers before the break and some after. I had to draw up a special plan for this. Another student was doing the Mocks much later, somewhere between St Patrick's Day and the Easter Break. They took place during March so a special plan was drawn up for him.

Where the Mocks are completed just before the mid-term, there has to be a bigger emphasis on rest and recovery. The period from the Christmas break to this break would have been very intense and very demanding. I would still be recommending a certain amount of work but not a huge amount. We must allow plenty of time for recovery.

Example 1: Seán, the First-Year Student

He is going away with his family for a mini-break. They will be away from early Wednesday morning to late on Saturday night. The following is my recommended schedule:

Saturday and Sunday at the start of the break – free for leisure/sport/family/rest activities.	
Monday	
Session 1	9.30 p.m. to 10.00 a.m.
Session 2	10.10 a.m. to 10.50 p.m.
Session 3	11.00 a.m. to 11.30 a.m.
Session 4	11.40 a.m. to 12.10 p.m.
Session 5	12.20 p.m. to 12.50 p.m.
Tuesday	
Session 1	10.00 a.m. to 10.30 a.m.
Session 2	10.40 a.m. to 11.10 a.m.
Session 3	11.20a.m. to 11.50 a.m.
Session 4	12.00 p.m. to 12.30 p.m.
Wednesday, Thursday, Friday and Saturday – away on family mini-break	
Sunday – free for leisure/sport/family/rest activities	

Note: I look for three 30-minute sessions on each of three days in the middle of the break for First-Year students. Because Seán is going away with his family for four days commencing on Tuesday, I am recommending that he does the nine 30-minute sessions over Monday and Tuesday.

Example 2: Susan, the Third-Year Student

She found the classes in the Dublin School of Grinds over Christmas really good. She is doing a full day of classes there on Thursday – 10.00 a.m. to 1.00 p.m. in the morning and 2.00 p.m. to 5.00 p.m. in the afternoon. Following is my recommended schedule:

Saturday, Sunday and Monday – free for leisure/sport/family/rest activities	
Tuesday	
Session 1	9.00 a.m. to 10.00 a.m.
Session 2	10.10 a.m. to 10.50 a.m.
Session 3	11.00 a.m. to 11.40 a.m.
Session 4	11.50 a.m. to 12.30 p.m.
Wednesday	
Session 1	2.00 p.m. to 3.00 p.m.
Session 2	3.10 p.m. to 3.50 p.m.
Session 3	4.00 p.m. to 4.40 p.m.
Session 4	4.50 p.m. to 5.30 p.m.
Thursday	
Classes in the Dublin School of Grinds:	
Session 1	10.00 am to 1.00 p.m.
Session 2	2.00 p.m. to 5.00 p.m.
Friday, Saturday and Sunday – free for leisure/sport/family/rest activities	

Note: I look for twelve hours school-related work for Third-Year students during this break. I normally look for it to be done during the three middle days of the break. Thursday is taken up with the classes in the Dublin School of Grinds so all the sessions at home are on Tuesday and Wednesday. For a bit of variety, the sessions on Tuesday are in the morning and on Wednesday, in the afternoon.

Example 3: Andrew, the Sixth-Year Student

He has rugby training on Tuesday and Thursday afternoons, 2.00 p.m. to 4.00 p.m. He is attending classes in the Grind School on Wednesday from 10.00 a.m. to 1.00 p.m. in the morning and from 2.00 p.m. to

5.00 p.m. in the evening. He has a Maths grind on Monday from 5.00 p.m. to 6.00 p.m. and an English one on Friday from 10.00 a.m. to 11.00 a.m. The following is my recommended schedule:

Saturday and Sunday at start of break – free for leisure/sport/family/rest activities	
Monday	
Maths grind	5.00 p.m. to 6.00 p.m.
Otherwise free	
Tuesday	
Session 1	9.00 a.m. to 11.00 a.m.
Session 2	11.10 a.m. to 12.10 p.m.
Session 3	12.20 p.m. to 1.20 p.m.
Rugby training	2.00 p.m. to 4.00 p.m.
Session 4	5.00 p.m. to 6.00 p.m.
Session 5	7.00 p.m. to 8.00 p.m.
Wednesday	
Dublin School of Grinds:	
Session 1	10.00 am to 1.00 p.m.
Session 2	2.00 p.m. to 5.00 p.m.
Thursday	
Session 1	9.00 a.m. to 11.00 a.m.
Session 2	11.10 a.m. to 12.10 p.m.
Session 3	12.20 p.m. to 1.20 p.m.
Rugby training	2.00 p.m. to 4.00 p.m.
Friday	
English grind	10.00 a.m. to 11.00 a.m.
Otherwise free	
Saturday and Sunday – free for leisure/sport/family/rest activities	

> **Note:** I look for eighteen hours of school-related work for Sixth-Year students. I want this to happen as much as possible in the middle of the break (on Tuesday, Wednesday and Thursday). The eighteen hours were broken up between classes in the Grind School (six hours), Maths and English grinds (two hours) and sessions at home (ten hours).

The Easter break

I refer to this time of the year as approaching the 'business end of things'. For Leaving Certificate students, it is a critical time. In the academic year we are looking at (2017/2018), the Easter break took place from Friday, 23 March to Monday, 9 April. The oral examinations took place during the first two weeks back after the Easter break.

I recommend that more time is allocated for school-related work than during the similar break at Christmas. For Leaving Certificate students, I recommend 64 hours of school-related work. With good planning, there can be plenty of time off as well. I suggest that the three weekends are free for leisure/sport/family/rest activities.

Where possible, the work in the first week is done Monday to Thursday inclusive and in the second week, Tuesday to Friday inclusive. On average, there should be eight hours done on each work day. This is the basis for working out the plan. Each individual's plan will be different. I recommend 30 hours of work for Junior Certificate students which equates to three hours per day and twelve hours at the Dublin School of Grinds.

For First-Year students, the amount of time remains the same as for the Christmas break: nine hours broken up into eighteen 30-minute sessions. The main objective with First-Year students is to get them used to allocating some time to school-related work in each of the four breaks. It should become clearer with the following three examples:

Example 1: Seán, a First-Year Student

Seán is going on a trip to the UK with his soccer club. He will be away from Wednesday of the first week to Easter Sunday. The following is my recommended schedule:

Saturday 24 and Sunday 25 March – free for leisure/sport/family/rest activities	
Monday, 26 March	
Session 1	10.00 a.m. to 10.30 a.m.
Session 2	10.40 a.m. to 11.10 a.m.
Session 3	11.20 a.m. to 11.50 a.m.
Tuesday, 27 March	
Session 1	4.00 p.m. to 4.30 p.m.
Session 2	4.40 p.m. to 5.10 p.m.
Session 3	5.20 p.m. to 5.40 p.m.
Wednesday 28 March, Thursday 29 March, Good Friday, Easter Saturday and Easter Sunday – Soccer trip to the UK.	
Easter Monday – free for leisure/sport/family/rest activities	
Tuesday, 3 April	
Session 1	10.00 a.m. to 10.30 a.m.
Session 2	10.40 a.m. to 11.10 a.m.
Session 3	11.20 a.m. to 11.50 a.m.
Session 4	12.00 p.m. to 12.30 p.m.
Wednesday, 4 April	
Session 1	2.00 p.m. to 2.30 p.m.
Session 2	2.40 p.m. to 3.10 p.m.
Session 3	3.20 p.m. to 3.50 p.m.
Session 4	4.00 p.m. to 4.30 p.m.

Thursday, 5 April	
Session 1	7.00 p.m. to 7.30 p.m.
Session 2	7.40 p.m. to 8.10 p.m.
Session 3	8.20 p.m. to 8.50 p.m.
Session 4	9.00 p.m. to 9.30 p.m.
Friday 6, Saturday 7 and Sunday 8 April – free for leisure/ sport/family/rest activities	

Note: Normally, we just want to have three 30-minute sessions on days when school-related work is being done. Because of the soccer trip to the UK, we had to include four sessions on the three days of the second week. It is good for students to realise that sacrifices have to be made sometimes to create opportunities like the soccer trip. First Year is a good time to learn about this.

Example 2: Susan, a Third-Year Student

Susan has a lot planned for the Easter break. She is involved in an Irish dancing Feis on Easter Saturday and Easter Sunday. She is attending classes in the Dublin School of Grinds on four days of the second week (Tuesday to Friday inclusive – mornings only – 10.00 a.m. to 1.00 p.m.). She has joined the Girl Guides and they are away for a day trip on Thursday of the first week. The following is my recommended schedule:

Saturday 24 and Sunday 25 March – free for leisure/sport/ family/rest activities.	
Monday, 26 March	
Session 1	9.30 a.m. to 10.30 a.m.
Session 2	10.40 a.m. to 11.20 a.m.
Session 3	11.30 a.m. to 12.10 p.m.
Session 4	12.20 p.m. to 1.00 p.m.

Tuesday, 27 March	
Session 1	2.00 p.m. to 3.00 p.m.
Session 2	3.10 p.m. to 3.50 p.m.
Session 3	4.00 p.m. to 4.40 p.m.
Session 4	4.50 p.m. to 5.30 p.m.
Wednesday, 28 March	
Session 1	9.30 p.m. to 10.30 a.m.
Session 2	10.40 p.m. to 11.20 a.m.
Session 3	11.30 a.m. to 12.10 p.m.
Session 4	12.20 p.m. to 1 p.m.
Thursday 29 – Day trip with the Girl Guides	
Good Friday – free for leisure/sport/family/rest activities	
Easter Saturday and Easter Sunday – involved in Irish dancing Feis	
Easter Monday – free for leisure/sport/family/rest activities	
Tuesday, 3 April	
Dublin School of Grinds	10.00 a.m. to 1.00 p.m.
Session 1	2.00 p.m. to 3.00 p.m.
Session 2	3.10 p.m. to 3.50 p.m.
Session 3	4.00 p.m. to 4.40 p.m.
Session 4	4.50 p.m. to 5.30 p.m.
Wednesday, 4 April	
Dublin School of Grinds	10.00 a.m. to 1.00 p.m.
Session 1	6.30 p.m. to 7.30 p.m.
Session 2	7.40 p.m. to 8.20 p.m.
Session 3	8.30 p.m. to 9.10 p.m.
Session 4	9.20 p.m. to 10.00 p.m.
Thursday, 5 April	
Dublin School of Grinds	10.00 a.m. to 1.00 p.m.
Session 1	2.00 p.m. to 3.00 p.m.

Session 2	3.10 p.m. to 3.50 p.m.
Session 3	4.00 p.m. to 4.40 p.m.
Session 4	4.50 p.m. to 5.30 p.m.
Friday, 6 April	
Dublin Grind School	10.00 a.m. to 1.00 p.m.
Saturday, 7 and Sunday, 8 April – free for leisure/sport/family/ rest activities.	

Note: The plan was to get 30 hours of school-related work done. This involved three days in the first week and four days in the second week. There was good balance with the three weekends off. There were four days over the long Easter weekend for leisure/ sport/family/rest activities. As I have mentioned before, the time off is just as important as the time spent at school-related work.

Example 3: Andrew, the Sixth-Year Student

Andrew has decided he is going to do mornings at supervised study in the school. Monday to Thursday inclusive in the first week and Tuesday to Friday inclusive in the second week (all 10.00 a.m. to 1.00 p.m.). His grinds in Maths and English are continuing. Two grinds each over the period – Maths (7.00 p.m. to 8.00 p.m. on Monday, 26 March and 5.30 p.m. to 6.30 p.m. on Friday, 6 April) and English (7.00 p.m. to 8.00 p.m. on Thursday, 29 March and 7.00 p.m. to 8.00 p.m. on Thursday, 5 April). The official rugby season is over but Andrew is still doing workouts in the gym. He is doing early morning workouts on Mondays, Wednesdays and Fridays (8.00 a.m. to 9.30 a.m.). The following is my recommended schedule:

Saturday 24 and Sunday 25 March – free for leisure/sport/family/ rest activities	
Monday, 26 March	
Workout in gym	8.00 a.m. to 9.30 a.m.
Supervised study in school	10.00 a.m. to 1.00 p.m.

Session 1	2.00 p.m. to 4.00 p.m.
Session 2	4.10 p.m. to 5.10 p.m.
Session 3	5.20 p.m. to 6.20 p.m.
Maths grind	7.00 p.m. to 8.00 p.m.
Session 4	8.10 p.m. to 9.10 p.m.
Tuesday, 27 March	
Supervised study in school	10.00 a.m. to 1.00 p.m.
Session 1	2.00 p.m. to 4.00 p.m.
Session 2	4.10 p.m. to 5.10 p.m.
Session 3	5.20 p.m. to 6.20 p.m.
Session 4	7.00 p.m. to 8.00 p.m.
Wednesday, 28 March	
Workout in gym	8.00 a.m. to 9.30 a.m.
Supervised study in school	10.00 a.m. to 1.00 p.m.
Session 1	2.00 p.m. to 4.00 p.m.
Session 2	4.10 p.m. to 5.10 p.m.
Session 3	5.20 p.m. to 6.20 p.m.
Session 4	7.00 p.m. to 8.00 p.m.
Thursday, 29 March	
Supervised study in School	10.00 a.m. to 1.00 p.m.
Session 1	2.00 p.m. to 4.00 p.m.
Session 2	4.10 p.m. to 5.10 p.m.
Session 3	5.20 p.m. to 6.20 p.m.
English grind	7.00 p.m. to 8.00 p.m.
Session 4	8.10 p.m. to 9.10 p.m.
Good Friday	
Workout in gym	8.00 a.m. to 9.30 a.m.
Free for leisure/sport/family/rest activities	

Easter Saturday, Easter Sunday and Easter Monday – free for leisure/sport/family/rest activities.	
Tuesday, 3 April	
Supervised study in school	10.00 a.m. to 1.00 p.m.
Session 1	2.00 p.m. to 4.00 p.m.
Session 2	4.10 p.m. to 5.10 p.m.
Session 3	5.20 p.m. to 6.20 p.m.
Wednesday, 4 April	
Workout in gym	8.00 a.m. to 9.30 a.m.
Supervised study in school	10.00 a.m. to 1.00 p.m.
Session 1	2.00 p.m. to 4.00 p.m.
Session 2	4.10 p.m. to 5.10 p.m.
Session 3	5.20 p.m. to 6.20 p.m.
Thursday, 5 April	
Supervised study in school	10.00 a.m. to 1.00 p.m.
Session 1	2.00 p.m. to 4.00 p.m.
Session 2	4.10 p.m. to 5.10 p.m.
Session 3	5.20 p.m. to 6.20 p.m.
English grind	7.00 p.m. to 8.00 p.m.
Friday, 6 April	
Workout in gym	8.00 a.m. to 9.30 a.m.
Supervised study in school	10.00 a.m. to 1.00 p.m.
Session 1	2.00 p.m. to 4.00 p.m.
Session 2	4.10 p.m. to 5.10 p.m.
Maths grind	5.30 to 6.30 p.m.
Session 3	7.00 p.m. to 8.00 p.m.
Saturday, 7 and Sunday, 8 April – free for leisure/sport/family/rest activities	

Note: We got the 64 hours fitted in with 24 hours in supervised study, four hours of grinds and 36 hours in the sessions at home (five hours each day in the first week and four hours each day in the second week). All the school-related work is on eight days with the other eight days for leisure/sport/family/rest activities. We were very happy with this balance.

Chapter 6

Breaking the Year Up into Periods

It is really important that each student focuses on the 'now' and doesn't look too far ahead. This can best be done by breaking the year up into distinct periods. This is a very important part of the overall plan for the year. For Leaving and Junior Certificate students, I break the year up into eleven periods. For First, Second and Fifth-Year students, there is just one period less. I leave out the second last period which is the lead-in to the start of the public examinations. It doesn't apply for non-examination classes as the normal school timetable will apply right up to the start of the summer house exams. The following is an example of how I break up the academic year for Junior and Leaving Certificate students:

The Eleven Periods

Period 1 – From the beginning of the year up to the start of the October mid-term break

This is a really important period as it sets the tone for the whole year. It is essential that a lot of thought goes into setting up the three schedules of work. This will bring real structure to what is going on outside of time spent in school. A huge part of it is accommodating sport/leisure/family/rest activities. This is essential for the health and well-being of each student. The first couple of weeks are vital in relation to having the best overall plan in place for the year. Any changes that need to be made should be done as early as possible. Also, each schedule of work is not written in stone. If something is not working, it must be changed. The schedules should be reviewed regularly during the year to make sure that they continue to work. Each student should settle in to their routine as quickly as possible. After a short while, they will have real trust in what is in place.

Period 2 – During the October mid-term break

There is a big emphasis here on sport/leisure/family/rest activities. The first term up to this point is always very demanding. It can take a lot out of students settling in to their routines after the long summer holidays. They need time to be able to re-charge their batteries. However, it is an ideal opportunity to get some school-related work done as well. I recommend that this work is done during the middle three days of the break (Tuesday, Wednesday and Thursday). This will give six days for sport/leisure/family/rest activities. A specific work schedule should be set up. It should include eighteen hours for Leaving Certificate students, twelve hours for Junior Certificate students and four-and-a-half hours for First-Year students. It may not be possible to do all of the school-related work in the middle three days. The specific work schedule should be drawn up in advance taking into consideration individual circumstances.

Period 3 – From the end of the October mid-term up to the start of the Christmas break

It's really important that students settle back quickly into their normal routines following the mid-term break. They must hit the ground running on the Monday following the break. They must apply themselves to the work schedules which they had in place for normal school days and weekends prior to the mid-term. By this stage, they should have total confidence in the schedules and commit totally to them. Again, if something is not working, it should be changed.

Period 4 – During the Christmas break

A big emphasis here should be on enjoying the Christmas festivities and the time around the New Year. However, time should be set aside for school-related work as well. Careful planning must take place so that all of this happens. I normally look for six days for school-related work. There are usually around sixteen days in this break which will leave ten days for sport/leisure/family/rest activities. This gives a really good balance. I would normally break up the six days of work up into two lots. I usually recommend three days in between Christmas and the New Year and the second three days between then and returning to school. Again, a specific work schedule should be in place. I look for a minimum of 36 hours work for Leaving Certificate students, 24 hours for Junior Certificate students and nine hours for First-Year students. It is essential that there is quality sport/leisure/family/rest time as the second term will be very demanding with the Mock examinations looming for Third- and Sixth-Year students.

Period 5 – From the end of the Christmas break to the start of the February mid-term

This is a really busy period, particularly for Junior and Leaving Certificate students with the Mock examinations featuring. Most schools have the Mocks during the two weeks immediately before the February mid-term. The most important aspect in relation to doing the Mocks is learning from the experience of doing them. To get the most out of them, you must prepare as well as possible for them. This is not easy as you will be attending normal classes in the build up. It takes very careful planning to incorporate adequate revision for the Mocks. The use of the examinations notebook gives you the best chance of achieving this. The six/seven weeks in this period are critical with regard to the overall preparations for the Junior and Leaving Certificate examinations.

Period 6 – During the February mid-term break

A bigger emphasis than normal is put on quality sport/leisure/family/ rest time here because of the very demanding period that preceded this. A minimum of six days off is recommended. Again, I look for any school-related work to be done during the middle three days. A minimum of twelve hours for Junior Certificate students, eighteen hours for Leaving Certificate students and four-and-a-half hours for First-Year students is suggested. In schools where the Mocks don't take place immediately before the break, a different plan will be needed. Also, where students have other commitments during this week, a specific work schedule has to be in place. Again, the importance of work schedules being drawn up in advance comes into play. Where possible, all sport/leisure/family/rest commitments are catered for.

Period 7 – From the end of the February mid-term to the start of the Easter break

Again, settling back into the normal routine quickly is important here. There will be a big emphasis in this period on doing follow-up work on the Mocks for Junior and Leaving Certificate students. Also, the orals normally take place during this period. Adequate time and attention must be given to preparing for them. However, students mustn't lose sight of keeping up with their normal work.

Period 8 – During the Easter break

A big emphasis here is on a good balance between fitting in quality sport/leisure/family/rest time and doing important school-related work. These two weeks are the final opportunity to get some much-needed rest and recovery time before the final run-in to the start of the Junior and Leaving Certificate examinations. With this in mind, I recommend eight days of work and eight days for sport/leisure/family/rest for Leaving Certificate students; seven days with work and nine days for sport/leisure/family/rest for Junior Certificate students; and six days with work and ten days with sport/leisure/family/rest for First-Year students. I suggest a total of 64 hours for Leaving Certificate students, 30 hours for Junior Certificate students and nine hours for First-Year students. As always, it is imperative that work schedules are prepared in advance. Again, individual needs should be catered for.

Period 9 – From the end of the Easter break up to when normal class periods cease

Hitting the ground running is essential on returning to school. Each student must apply him/herself to the work schedules for normal school days and weekends. At this stage, teachers can be winding down a little and students can be left to their own devices to a large degree. There can be a lot of distractions with formal school drawing to a close. Each student must have tunnel vision and focus on what they have to do. They must do what they can to stick with their overall plan. One of the big distractions will be the Graduation. It is a very important event so must be embraced. However, students must be able to focus on what they have to do right up to it and immediately after it.

Period 10 – From when normal classes cease up to the Monday before the Junior and Leaving Certificate commence

This can be a minefield. It is normally about two weeks for Leaving Certificate students and a week for Junior certificate students. Students can lose their way a bit here. It probably applies more to Sixth-Year students as they suddenly realise that they are more or less finished with school. A special plan/work schedule must be put in place during this period. I recommend that it should include more than they would have spent at school on a daily basis. I suggest a minimum of eight hours per weekday for Leaving Certificate students and six hours for Junior Certificate students. They should create adequate sport/leisure/family/rest time over the three weekends in the lead-in to the exams – maybe four hours of work on each of the Saturdays and Sundays for the Leaving Certificate students and three hours for the Junior Certificate students.

Period 11 – During the Junior and Leaving Certificate examinations themselves

A final revision plan must be put in place that will work through the exams. It must be linked to the examinations timetable. Students should get into 'exam mode' the day before they start. The objective for each student is to be in the form of their life for each paper that they have to sit. For this to happen, revision the night/day before should be gentle and light enough. Advantage should be taken of gaps in the exam timetable – days/half-days off, etc. Also, weekends during the examinations. A special revision plan should be in place on a daily basis. As mentioned already, it should include adequate rest and recovery to re-charge the batteries. The plan should work right up to the last paper that each student has to sit. There can be a tendency to take the foot a little off the pedal as the end nears. This must be avoided at all costs. The last paper is just as important as the ones that have gone before. For Leaving Certificate students, it just might make the difference to take the student over the line in relation to the points they need.

I cannot emphasise enough the importance of breaking the year up into the **eleven periods**. It is a great way of getting each student to **focus on the 'now'**. A lot of thought goes into planning the year. Each student can see clearly what lies ahead. This is a really big part of the overall plan. A lot of time and effort goes into getting things right for each individual student for the year ahead. Students know that if they commit to the plan consistently through each period, they stand the best chance of realising their potential in the end-of-year examinations. They will now have the confidence to get on with their lives on a day-to-day basis knowing that they have the best plan in place to meet their individual needs and wants.

Chapter 7

Realising One's Potential in Examinations

Many students can feel very intimidated about examinations. As a result of this, they don't perform to their potential. It is normal to feel a little nervous about the prospect of doing exams. This will happen with any important occasion that is coming up. A student should not be too nervous as it will affect their performance. They should try to develop a positive attitude towards sitting examinations. This must be done at an early stage. We must work on this in First Year. Teachers and parents must help them to see that exams/tests are opportunities to show off what they know. It is like the actors preparing for their first night or the team preparing for the big match. This is what all the hard work is about. It is all about making all our preparations the best they can be. This puts us in the strongest possible position to perform to the best of our ability. There is no guarantee that the really well-prepared team is going to win the match. However, by preparing really well, they put themselves in the best possible position to succeed.

It is exactly the same way with examinations. The better your preparations are, the more chance you have of achieving top grades. It is all about doing your best as that is all that anyone can ask of you. Let the results take care of themselves. It all comes down to having the best plan in place for each stage of your secondary school life, trusting your plan and committing to it to the best of your ability. In reality, you are preparing for the Leaving Certificate examinations from the first day you walk into secondary school. Some key issues that affect performance in examinations are outlined, below.

Preparation

As mentioned above, you really start preparing for the Leaving Certificate examination on the first day you start secondary school. Everything you do throughout the following six years has an influence on what you will achieve in these examinations. However, you must always focus on what is happening in the current moment and not look too far ahead. You must prepare as best you can for each and every day at school. By doing this, you are preparing in the best way possible for any examinations you will face in the future.

You must put a plan in place for preparing for each exam you are going to undertake. First-Year students need help with this. They must realise that preparing well will put them in a good position to perform well. They should see that working hard for something will make them want to be rewarded. This comes in the form of good results from the exams. When they see this, it will help them to look forward to receiving this recognition in the form of good results. Once they see that preparing well in the lead-up to examinations leads to the best results, they will want to do this. For them, it is a little on a regular basis. Having a definite schedule for them at an early stage is the best way forward. After a while, they will become used to it. With a timetable in place like the one in school which they have to follow, it will just be part of their regular routine.

In the same way that we plan for our regular school-related work, we must also do the same when preparing for examinations. All the general ongoing school work is long-term preparation for examinations. As well as this, we must prepare for each exam we have to sit. A special revision plan must be put in place for each examination. There should be one for the lead-in to the exam as well as one for during the examination itself. All the heavy detailed work should be done well in advance of the start of the examination in question.

The revision during the examinations should be of a more gentle nature. The whole purpose of good preparation for exams is that the student is in the best possible condition to perform to their ability during each paper. This is where your own short concise notes play an important role. We will look at this in detail later on in this section. Your revision plan for during the examinations should be closely linked with the exam timetable. You will be going over material each night to do with papers you will be sitting the next day. As we have already mentioned, this work should not be too intense or too detailed. You should look closely at the timetable for the exams weeks before they commence. There will be some vital revision/preparation that will have to be done in the lead-in rather than the night before. Effective planning is essential here to make sure preparations are the best they can be.

If your preparation has been the best it can be, you will be in a really strong position to perform to your potential in the examinations. This must happen in each subject. It is a long process taking up to two years. It all comes back to planning well, trusting your plan and committing to it. If some part of the plan is not working, you must change it. Decisiveness is key here and it is not wise to persist with something that is not working. You want to reach the point just before the start of the Leaving Certificate where you have total confidence in your ability to perform in each of your subjects.

Note: 'Fail to plan and you plan to fail.'

Time Management

Time management is a crucial area in every aspect of school life. It is particularly crucial with regard to performing well in examinations. Optimum use of time is essential if you are going to perform to the best of your ability. Making the best use of time at your disposal is vital if you are to achieve top grades. A huge amount of effort goes into becoming competent at using time.

One must become very disciplined about it. It starts with our general school life. We must be punctual at all times. We must arrive in good time for everything we are involved in – being on time for school in the morning, being on time for each class period, being on time for each session of supervised study in school, being on time for each session of school-related work at home, being on time for the rugby/hockey training session etc. The list is endless. There is a discipline in all of this. The same when talking about our use of time when doing things. Being a good timekeeper is essential if we are to use our time in the best way possible. We must get it right in our general school work first. We have only a certain amount of time to do things. We must be aware of this when we are doing our homework each evening. We must plan our work sessions well so that we get what we have to do done within the time available to us. By doing this well in our school-related work at supervised study and at home, we are preparing well for doing it in exams. It is not just about finishing something in the time allowed, it is more about using the time in the best way possible. A lot of work must be done in advance of sitting examinations if we are to perfect this. We look at many of these issues in this section.

This is an area where parents can help their children during the early part of secondary school. Rather than just getting homework done and out of the way, parents need to help students to plan sessions better so that they are using the time they have allocated in the best way possible. It's important to make them aware of how important time management is. Students should work on their time management skills when they are doing their regular school-related work. Get it right here and it will spill over into the work produced during exams. Students should reach the point when they know exactly how long they can spend on each question of every paper. This must happen when we are preparing for the Junior and Leaving Certificate examinations.

There is an awful lot of writing in many subjects in the Leaving Certificate examinations. There is also a danger that you can run over the time you should spend when answering a particular question. The first part in getting this right is **knowing the time you should spend on answering each question** in every subject. A lot of preparation must go into this.

The next part is being disciplined and vigilant in relation to implementing it under exam conditions. A lot of practice is required to perfect it. Doing **questions from past papers** is critical here. As you are getting closer to the Leaving Certificate examinations, you need to time yourself. Where you are running over, you must identify where you can save time. In my main subject of Accounting, students sometimes lost track of time because they were so engrossed in trying to find a difference they had. Why is it not balancing? Another good example is when doing an Essay. Students become so engrossed in the storyline of their essay that they lose track of time. It is a really key area in relation to you performing to your potential. There are many aspects to time management that must be addressed.

> **Note:** Time is one of the most precious commodities of all. We must not be wasteful with it.

Having All the Basic Accessories You Need

This requires being consistently well organised at all times. It is one thing having all you need at the very start of sitting an examination. It is another thing making sure you have everything you need right to the very end of the last paper. It seems a very obvious requirement but, nonetheless, very important. Students can be in danger of becoming a little careless as they progress through the examinations. They may not be as attentive to such details as they near the end of the examination. With regard to the public examinations, I recommend that you **have a checklist of accessories needed for each paper you will sit**. This will make sure that there is consistency right to the very end of the last paper. Even though we are only talking about the basic accessories required for doing each paper, it must be given the attention it deserves. It is another example of how important basic details are. 'Take care of the little things and the big picture will take care of itself.' To get this right in exams, you must pay attention to it on a day-to-day basis. **Make sure you are organised on a daily basis in relation to having all the accessories in your bag**.

During my years as principal, I had many students coming to me looking to borrow items they had forgotten. This would normally happen towards the end of the Leaving and Junior Certificate examinations each year. Even the best of students can become a little careless towards the end. I would always have had stocks of items they were likely to need. However, I always felt that this panic just before the start of an examination was not ideal preparation for performing to their potential. Students must be in total control of what they need to have with them. They must take total responsibility for this and not be depending on others. They must have the same routine for checking right through to the very last paper. Such disorganisation could make the difference between achieving the points you require or just coming up short. It can come down to small margins at the end.

> **Note:** Take nothing for granted. It is just as important to check that you have everything you need for the last exam as it was for the first.

Compiling Your Own Short Concise Notes

This is the best type of school-related work. It is a very important part of the long-term preparations for sitting examinations. It is very constructive school-related work leading to something very valuable when it comes to revising for examinations. The process involved in compiling notes is very rewarding in itself. You have to understand the material you are working on before you put it in a short concise form. You eventually end up with a valuable set of notes for revision purposes. I maintain that you can make meaningful notes in every subject. I recommend to the students I work with to make their own notes on all handouts that they receive. I am not just referring to making notes on subject material covered. This is just one important part of note making. The notes made might be on technique for answering particular questions. It might be on the recommended content for different essays.

For students preparing for the public examinations, I suggest that they compile their own notes on the layout, marking scheme, etc of each paper they are going to sit. The process of doing this is extremely productive as the thoroughness of it all will ensure that you retain a lot of what you have worked on. It also provides you with a real focus when you are doing your school-related work outside of homework. When students are focusing on answering questions from past papers, I recommend that they make notes on the key aspects in each answer. Each student can develop their own personal style for doing this. You are eventually coming up with all the material/information you need for final preparations for sitting the exams.

I also recommend that students make their own notes from handouts they get. The following points are important when working on compiling your own set of short concise notes:

- You must first decide on how you are you are going to keep the notes. **Ring binders are very useful**. They enable you to add to your notes at any time.

- A big effort should be made to ensure the quality is the best it can be at all times. **Notes can be done out roughly first before you arrive at the final article**.

- You should **make your own notes on any handouts** you receive. There is nothing like having your own notes in your own handwriting.

- Part of your plan should be to **summarise** your original notes for revision purposes before examinations. You can eventually have **bullet points** which are excellent for final revision.

- Notes can be made in **all subjects**. In subjects like Maths and Accounting, the emphasis maybe on formulae, definitions and techniques for answering questions.

- Note-making should eventually be **linked with questions from past papers**. It should include having notes on the layout/content of examination papers in all subjects. This would include details of the instructions of each paper including the marking schemes. This is an important part of what I call becoming 'street wise' with regard to doing exams.

- Each section of notes should include **sample answers** to examination questions on that particular material. Notes can be made on key areas for answering such questions. A big effort should be put into time management. Specific notes can be made on how to make best use of time available for answering each question.

- Returned scripts from **tests/examinations** can be linked to notes. You could include a note on areas you fell down in. Having done work/research, etc, you can then include the correct answer as part of your notes. You will develop your own individual way of doing this.

- You must always be able to **add to your notes**. As mentioned above, the ring binder system is ideal for this. There may be additional information to be added to your original notes. Linking your notes to questions from past papers is a good example here. It is an ongoing process.

- The process for compiling your own notes involves **five stages**: Stage 1 – Making your original notes; Stage 2 – Summarising them; Stage 3 – Bullet Points; Stage 4 – Linking them to test/ examination questions; and Stage 5 – Adding to your notes on an ongoing basis.

Note: You can make notes on everything!

Focus and Concentration

We must first of all work on our focus and concentration in everything we do on a daily basis. It is easy to focus on things that we like. Some students will say to me that they have no problem with focus and concentration in certain classes or when working on certain subjects. In the areas where we have **difficulty** with our focus and concentration, we must **identify** why this is happening and **try to eliminate the distractions that cause the problems**.

It might be that we find a particular subject somewhat boring. In such a case, we have to be determined to overcome this. We might need to **prioritise extra work** in this subject to try and generate additional interest. It might be that a particular teacher's style is not to your liking. It is down to you to overcome this attitude and make the required progress despite your opinion.

This is where you need **tunnel vision**. You must be determined to succeed despite your views on the set-up in place. Good focus and concentration during examinations is essential if we are to realise our potential. There is only a limited amount of time in each examination so we must take full advantage of every minute available. We must work on our focus and concentration when doing our school-related work in school and at home. We must work on it in these places first and it will spill over into when we are sitting examinations.

When our preparations for the exams are the best they could be, it will be easier to get our focus and concentration up to the required level. It becomes more difficult to focus well as we become tired. I refer to this as striving to achieve the required levels of fitness for sitting examinations. When we reach this point, we will have the necessary **stamina** to be able to focus and concentrate well right to the last minute of the last exam. This only comes with hard work and practice under examination-type pressure. You should assess the level of your focus and concentration on a day-to-day basis and identify areas of concern. You should change things under your control that would make the level of your concentration better.

You should do the same after each examination that you sit. Identify where your focus and concentration was below what it should have been, establish what the cause was and make sure that the same thing won't happen again. We must make sure that the level of our focus and concentration is the best it can be throughout every examination. We only have a limited amount of time to complete our answers so we cannot afford any lapses in concentration.

An important part of getting our focus and concentration the best it can be during the Leaving and Junior Certificate examinations is having a **good daily routine**. Make sure we arrive in **plenty of time** for the start of each paper. On the days when you have two papers, plan well what you are going to do in between. There could be up to two hours here. Part of it might be spent on some **light revision** from your specially prepared notes. It is important to have a **healthy lunch** that will give you the necessary energy to cope with the afternoon paper. Also, get some **fresh air** to clear your head. Try to avoid any energetic sports activities that might drain you of energy. All this must be planned well so that you are in peak condition for each paper.

Getting your focus and concentration right for the first paper is vital. It can set the tone for the rest of the exams. Once English Paper 1 is put on your desk and you are given the go-ahead to start, you must have tunnel vision. **Shut everything else out of your mind except the work at hand.** This intense focus must last until the final minute of each exam. Greater effort is required towards the end of each paper when fatigue can set in. Also, during examinations towards the end of the timetable. It requires total commitment and determination to keep focus and concentration consistently at the highest possible level.

> **Note:** We will only realise our potential in examinations when our focus and concentration are at their highest levels.

Becoming Familiar with the Layout of All Papers

When it comes to performing well in examinations, it is very important to feel comfortable from the word go. You must be in control of the things you can control. Being very familiar with the layout of all papers is one of these things that you can be in control of. If a really tough question comes up or something you really prepared for well doesn't appear, you can do nothing about this. You just have to deal with it as best you can. If you are shocked by an aspect to do with the basic layout of the paper, that is totally different. This could have been avoided.

Time and effort must be made available to do the necessary preparatory work. I have found that some extremely strong students have been negligent in this regard. They become experts in relation to all aspects of their subject areas but can take for granted a simple thing like **knowing the layout of each paper**. There is much more to achieving a top grade than just knowing your subject material inside out. I refer to becoming 'street wise' in relation to performing well in examinations. There are many aspects to this and being familiar with the layout of papers is one of them. You want to avoid being shocked in any way at the start of an exam. There are certain things you can't control but there are definite things you can control and this is one of them.

The layout of some papers can be complicated. The Geography one springs to mind in the Leaving Certificate. Every student is capable of doing what is required in relation to becoming familiar with layouts. They should **look over every paper going back at least five years**. Make sure you are familiar with every aspect and angle to it. It is a really important part of being totally prepared for each exam.

> **Note:** Allocate time to work on becoming familiar with the layout of every paper you will be sitting.

Knowing the Marking Scheme for Each Paper

Every student should be aware of the mark for each question relative to the total for the paper. If you are looking for a top grade, this will have a big influence on the questions you choose to do. In the Leaving Certificate examination, if you are looking for a H1 (90% and over), you will have to do the questions that carry the highest marks. You must have a definite **strategy** in relation to this. It is an important part of being 'street wise' in relation to doing exams. I also believe that **marks can be linked to time management**. They can be **used to determine how long you should spend answering each question**. It is not the only way to do it but, in my opinion, it is a good way. My main teaching subject was Accounting. I used this method very effectively with my students. I was very strict with them with regard to **how much time to spend on each answer**. The method is very simple. You simply **put the marks for the question over the total marks for the whole paper multiplied by the total time for the overall paper.**

This gives you the time in minutes that you should spend answering this question. If the allocated marks for a given question is 130, the total mark for the paper is 400 marks and the total time allowed is 3 hours (180 minutes), you should spend 58 minutes on this question:

I told students that **under no circumstances were they to run over**. I used to joke with them and say that they should have a little 'alarm clock' on their desk that would go off. They were then to move on. Of course, they couldn't do this but it helped get through to them the importance of sticking to time. I used to **take a little time off the calculated figure for each question so that there was time to look over things at the end**. An approach like this emphasises the importance of managing time well. I always got my students to record the time it took when they were doing questions for homework. My thinking here was that if they were disciplined in relation to time when doing their homework, they would be the same when answering questions in exams.

It is vital that you know the marks that are going for every part of every question. As I have mentioned before, it can come down to very small margins in relation to you achieving the points required for your selected course at third-level. A very important part of this is being totally aware of all the marks available throughout the paper. It will form a crucial part of your strategy with regard to what to answer and what to leave out.

> **Note:** It is all about using time in the most productive way. A lot of time and effort must go into knowing what marks are available for each section. You can then plot out how you will go about achieving the marks you are targeting.

Being Familiar with the Instructions for Each Paper

I corrected papers for many years for the public examinations. My subjects were Business Studies at Junior Certificate level and Accounting at Leaving Certificate level. It used to amaze me how many students would ignore the instructions. **The most common mistake was not doing the required number of questions in each section.** It might be that students would only answer one question from a section when they were specifically asked to do two. Or, when asked to do only one question in a section, they might do two. In the latter case, the time spent on the second question is totally wasted as they were not asked to do it. It also means that they would have been all over the place in relation to time. They would have to rush things when doing other questions because they wasted time on this. All this could have been avoided if they had become **familiar with the instructions on past papers**. Time and effort must be set aside for this as an important part of the overall preparations for the exams.

> **Note:** Take nothing for granted. Do the necessary preparation so that silly mistakes will be avoided.

Read Questions a Few Times Before Answering Them

A little time spent doing this before you start can save you time through the course of answering each question. **It is really important that you are very clear on what the question is looking for.** You need to know the **angle** they are looking for. Rushing in to answer a question is not the best tactic. There must be no doubt in your mind about the content to be included.

Sometimes you see what you want to see rather than what is actually there. I learned about this the hard way many years ago when I was doing my own Leaving Certificate. It happened on Paper 1 in Irish. I had learned a particular essay (that was hotly tipped to come up) off by heart. It was 'A Footballer Tells His Life Story'. It was around the time of the Soccer World Cup in 1966 so the topic was expected. I was depending a lot on it coming up so it was the first thing I looked for. My prayers were answered when I saw it there. At least, I thought I saw it there. I jumped straight in to do it without reading the topics a second time and was really pleased with my essay and the way I answered the rest of the paper. When chatting with a few of my friends after the exam, one of them asked me what essay did I do. I told him I did 'A Footballer Tells His Life Story'. 'You fool,' he said. 'That was "A Football Tells Its Life Story"'. I was devastated, to say the least. I was sure I had failed and that I only had myself to blame. Not only that. It severely dented my confidence as it was one of the first exams.

I learned two very important lessons that day. Firstly, **read over questions a few times before answering**. In my case above, I saw what I wanted to see rather than what was actually there. I was banking on it so much that I jumped to conclusions. Secondly, from that day on, I never discussed an exam with anyone else once it was over. I have always recommended this approach to my students over the years. **The minute you walk out of an exam, you move on to the next one.** You can't influence the one you have just done anymore. So, move on!

> **Note:** Slow things down at the beginning of each exam. Spend time reading questions carefully so that you are in no doubt about what the question is looking for.

Have a Definite Plan for Tackling Each Paper

This follows on from a really thorough preparation. You must have a definite plan for tackling each paper. If you are very familiar with everything you are going to face, you can come up with a specific strategy. You won't know the specific questions that are going to be there but you will know the areas that will appear in each section.

Spending a few minutes looking over the whole paper at the start is essential. You will have a broad outline of your plan coming into the exam. This initial check will enable you to firm up on your strategy. Having gone through the content in the overall paper, you may have to adjust your plan a little as a result of specific questions that are there. Following these few minutes, you will then have your definite plan for tackling the paper.

You might **list the order in which you are going to tackle the questions** on your rough work. The few minutes you spend doing this will save you time later on. You then have to be very decisive in what you do through the course of the exam. You will know the amount of time you are going to spend on each question. You have to be really disciplined here and avoid running over time on any answer. All the practice you have put in doing questions from past papers will pay off now. You will have total confidence in your plan which will allow you to perform to the best of your ability. Students who are looking for a **top grade** (H1 – over 90%) **can't afford to leave even a small part of a question out**. This forward planning and discipline will give students the best chance of achieving the required outcome.

> **Note:** Being decisive and in control is essential if you are to realise your potential in each exam.

Be Calm and Collected about What Appears to Be a Difficult Paper

Every student hopes that the questions will be to their liking. This doesn't always happen. You can be sure that at least a few papers will be **more difficult than what you were hoping for, and some will turn** out to be nothing like what you were expecting. You have to be able to cope with this. Some students don't react well to what appears to be a difficult paper. I can understand students being disappointed if questions they were banking on are not there. Some students become really negative when this happens. Their **confidence** is down and they tend to struggle for the duration of that exam. This doesn't have to happen. The attitude should be **'I don't particularly like what has come up but I am determined to do everything I can over the next three hours to get the best grade I can.'** It is all about attitude here. In situations like this, you have to be prepared to dig deep. The first thing you do is you look for something you are comfortable to start with. Your game plan may have to change to suit the circumstances.

Once you get started, the initial shock will disappear. Sometimes, **what appears to be a really difficult paper at first glance may not be that bad.** Also, a difficult paper is the same for everyone. Certain questions may be marked easier. I remember occasions when the chief examiner contacted me to say that students were struggling with answering certain questions and we were to be more lenient with allocating marks. You have to develop a **toughness** in relation to facing a more difficult paper than you were expecting. You can't just be banking on certain questions coming up. It helps to anticipate that this might happen. **You need to have thought out how you will react to something like this happening.** The important thing is that you remain positive and confident that you can cope under difficult circumstances.

> **Note:** Be prepared for all questions not being to your liking and don't let a tough question dent your confidence.

Use Rough Work as an Aid

The use of rough work during an exam should not be underestimated. It can be of benefit in many ways. **I often gave marks for information on rough work** that I wouldn't have given for what was on the official answer book.

My main subject was Accounting. An example would be as follows: 10 marks were allocated for the sales figure in the final accounts. There might have been a number of adjustments that needed to be made to the figure on the exam paper. Some students would show their workings on rough work. I often gave the full marks to a student whose method/technique was correct but the final figure was wrong due to a simple adding mistake. **If the student didn't show their workings, they would have got no marks for this.** This is only one example.

There are lots of ways that **rough work can be really beneficial**. You could list the order you are going to do questions in. If you had just memorised a few definitions before the exam, you could write them down on the rough work sheets at the start. Also, it is a great way of **establishing the structure of answers**. A good example would be in firming up on the structure for an essay: What will I have in the introduction? What points will I have in the main body of the essay? What will I have in the conclusion? It is also good for checking the correct spelling for a word.

Each individual student will have ways of using rough work that suits them. **For practice, it is good to use it when doing questions from past papers.** Make it part of your routine in your preparatory work in supervised study or at home. **Always hand up your rough work with your official answer book.**

> **Note:** Rough work can be a great help when sitting examinations. A lot of thought must go into how best to use it.

Start Each Paper with a Question You Are Comfortable With

It is always important to get off to a good start. It sets the tone for what is to follow. My advice is to **start with something you are strong at**. This will then give you the confidence to deal with more difficult questions that will follow. It is all part of having a definite plan. It can be down to individual preferences as well.

I worked with a student recently who wanted to start with his most difficult question on Paper 1 of Higher Level Maths. He was determined to do it this way. His thinking was to get it done while everything was fresh in his mind. I went along with that because he had given it a lot of thought and he felt that it was the best strategy for him.

The important thing is that each student has a **definite plan for each paper**. My thinking is that it can be very difficult to recover from a poor start. It can be hard to clear your mind of something going badly wrong. You have to make sure that you are aware of the consequences of something going wrong and how you will recover. It is all about seeing yourself in that situation and knowing how you will deal with it.

> **Note:** Ideally, it is great to get off to a strong start. If it doesn't happen, you must be ready to deal with that as well.

Be Very Clear on What You Are Going to Include in Each Answer

There is a tendency when sitting exams to rush too quickly into answering questions. You need to be very clear on what you are going to write. Reading the question a few times before answering is essential. Know exactly what angle the question is looking for. There is a danger of misreading questions if you don't take care in identifying what is being looked for. As mentioned earlier, rough work can be a great help here. Once you are clear on what you are looking for, **it is a good tactic to write down in your rough work the main points you want to include in your answer.** This will bring real structure to your answer. It will avoid the temptation to waffle on too much. A little time thinking about what to include in your answer will save time in the long run. Being really organised like this will make sure that your answer is of a high quality. It is all about being in control and making sure that each answer is of the highest quality possible.

> **Note:** It is very important that your key points jump out from the paper to the examiner.

Presenting Your Answers to the Highest Standard Possible

When it comes to performing well in examinations, **it is essential that your answers are presented to a high standard.** To be able to do this in examinations, you have to work on it in your regular work in school, at supervised study and at home. If you tend to be a little careless with your work in general, it will be the same in examinations and may even be worse. It should be a priority to present work to the highest quality at all times. **You must take a pride in the work you are doing at all times. Your writing doesn't have to be beautiful. It just has to be legible and clear**. This is a very important aspect of good exam technique.

I often think back to my years of correcting the public examinations. Following the exam conference in Athlone, I would return home with my sack of papers ready to commence my work. I knew that there would be long days ahead throughout the month of July with early-morning starts. I used to start each morning before 7.00 a.m. and work until 7.00 p.m. in the evening to meet deadlines. My memory is that **well-presented scripts were much easier to correct. Points would jump out at you off the page and marks could be allocated very easily.** The opposite happened with material badly presented. You had to look very hard to identify where marks could be given. There is no doubt in my mind that **well-presented answers achieve higher marks**. This might make the difference in taking you on to the **next grade**. It can be on very small margins at the end of the day. How you present your work in examinations is something that is totally in your control. It is something that you really have to work on. It starts with you focusing on it when you are doing your homework, compiling your notes, answering questions from past papers, doing class tests, etc.

Note: Your writing and general presentation is something you have to work really hard at. The rewards are high when you reach the required standards.

Consistency of Work/Presentation throughout Each Exam

The quality of your work in examinations must be high right to the end of each exam. There must be **consistency** through each paper. It is easy to start off with your writing/presentation at a high level in relation to how it is presented. The difficulty is with **maintaining it to the end of each exam**. I refer to this as 'fitness' with regard to doing exams. It is not easy to keep this up for the duration of each exam. There is a huge amount of writing to be done in many subjects. To be able to cope with this when the pressure comes on in exams, a lot of **practice** must take place in advance. Exam situations must be simulated for such practice to be effective. Students only have one full-scale practice of the Leaving Certificate when they do the Mock examinations. This is not enough. I used to give my Leaving Certificate students a second Mock during the Easter break just to give them another full-scale practice. Students must take on this responsibility themselves by **testing their 'fitness'** in relation to maintaining a very high standard of work/presentation right to the very end. It must be part of their overall plan for preparing for the Leaving Certificate. They should be their own hardest critic on this. Expect very high standards and do what is necessary to deliver on this.

> **Note:** The work you do in the last five minutes of an exam is just as important as at any stage earlier on. In fact, it may be more important.

Use the Full Length of Each Exam, No Matter What the Circumstances Are

We spoke of optimum use of time earlier under time management. A very important part of this is working up to the very end of each exam. There should never be a reason for leaving an examination early. Each paper is designed to take the allocated time. Students should make sure to use all of it in the best way possible. This **includes reading over the entire paper** before you start, reading each question **a few times** before you start answering that question, **planning the structure** of each answer before you begin it, etc. All of this has been mentioned earlier. **Having a strong finish to each paper is essential**. For me, this would be **allowing for a few minutes at the end to go over everything**. You might suddenly spot something that needs to be adjusted which could mean additional marks. This could make the difference of moving a candidate up to the next grade.

During my years as principal, myself and the deputy principal used to keep a record of students who left the centre before the end of exams in the Leaving Certificate. We used to ask them their reason for leaving early and they would say it was because they were finished. We knew that they hadn't achieved to the extent of their potential because of departing early. When the results came out, we always found this to be the case. They would have done alright but below what they were capable of. They failed to make optimum use of the time at their disposal. This is another example of failing to take maximum advantage of something that is totally within your control.

> **Note:** The time allocated to do an exam in is given for a reason. Make sure to take full advantage of it.

Overall Approach to Doing Tests and Examinations

I have worked with many students who simply believe that they are not good in test and examination situations. They have convinced themselves that they just don't perform well under the pressure of exams. I noticed this too during my years as a teacher. Some students with great potential didn't produce the goods in tests and exams. I could see what they were capable of through their work and participation in class. It frustrated me a lot that certain students didn't perform to their ability under exam conditions and there was very little I could do on an individual basis with students like this.

This was one of the main reasons I set up my One2One Mentoring Service thirteen years ago. I knew I could make a difference for individual students if I could work with them on a one-to-one basis. I won't accept a student telling me that they just don't perform well in exams.

Instead **I put a huge emphasis on preparing students for performing to their ability in exams**. I consider this aspect to be equally as important as knowing your subject material. A lot of time and effort must go into this preparation if you are to do yourself justice in exams. I have touched on all the relevant key areas already in this section and in addition I have a handout I give to students I work with to help them with exam technique, which is reproduced in this chapter. It has eighteen simple basic points that they must apply if they are going to realise their potential in exams. Students use these bullet points as a checklist. And they are encouraged to work on this in the period leading up to the Leaving Certificate. The objective is to be able to tick each point off in advance of sitting the exams.

I get students to look forward to sitting exams. One thing I say to each student is that this is your opportunity to show what you can achieve. Use this opportunity. If students have prepared really well in every way, there is absolutely no reason why they should be afraid. This is what all the preparation has been for.

> **Note:** If a student is negative in any way about an exam, this must be addressed. The reason for the negativity must be identified and tackled.

Chapter 8

Mindset

Attitude

A student's overall attitude is very important. A positive attitude must be in place if the required level of progress is to be achieved. It is essential to start off each school year in a positive frame of mind. This is especially important at the start of Sixth Year. Students are about to embark on the most important year of their school lives. Their futures will be determined to a large degree on what they achieve during their Leaving Certificate year. Targeted grades will be set in each subject which in turn will determine the total points they can achieve. This desired outcome will only be achieved with a positive attitude and a total commitment to the plan in place. This must happen consistently through the year.

My objective for each student I work with is always for each one to be able to say: 'When I walk out of the last exam, I can look back and say, I couldn't have done anymore.' If they can say this, there is a really good chance they will achieve their targeted grades. I would go further than that and say that they normally do. For this to happen, there must be a positive attitude consistently through the year.

Of course, there will be ups and downs along the way. All of us have bad days from time to time. We must be able to put a day like that behind us and resume normal service as quickly as possible. This is where the positive attitude kicks in. We must make sure that we don't lose out in any way as a result of a bad day or experience. Extra work may be necessary to catch up on anything that we missed out on. This is where good planning comes in. Whatever has to be done doesn't have to be attended to immediately. As long as you get around to it at some stage, that is fine. This is where the 'work in progress' notebook I recommend comes in very helpful. I cover this in detail in Chapter 9.

Each individual student has to take responsibility for what has to be done. Again, the overall attitude is key here. For everything to function well, our attitude must be right. We must make sure that this is in place at the beginning of the year and remains for the duration. With a positive attitude, we can achieve anything.

> **Note:** A positive attitude is essential to give students a real chance of succeeding.

Strengths

Each student has many strengths. Sometimes, students are not aware of the strengths they have. It is a matter of identifying them and making full use of them. Strengths should never be taken for granted. I worked with a student a few years ago who was really strong at Technical Drawing. He achieved an A in the Junior Certificate in Technical Graphics. In every test and exam through Fifth and Sixth Year, he always got an A1 (over 90%), the equivalent in the old grading system of the H1 now. This included an A1 in the Mock Leaving Certificate. Unknown to me, he took his foot a little off the pedal in Technical Drawing in the run up to the Leaving Certificate exams. He became a little complacent and over confident. The end result was a B1 (between 80 and 85%). He took it for granted that he would continue to get an A1. It was a very costly mistake as he just missed out on the points for his chosen third-level course. He admitted to me afterwards that he had eased off a little in his work for this subject.

I use this as an example with all of my students of the importance of never taking anything for granted. You must always be determined to become even stronger in areas where you already are strong. The least you should achieve is to maintain the same high standards. Some of the students I work with are 'early-morning people'. I would include early morning sessions for these in their work schedules. I consider this to be playing to their strengths. Some students are not good early in the morning so you would avoid including such sessions in their plan. It is all about identifying your unique strengths and playing to these in your plans.

> **Note:** Every student is different. The strengths of each individual student must be identified and brought to the fore.

Weaknesses

Weaknesses must be identified and action taken to address them. Every time I meet a student, I ask them to tell me what their two 'weaker' subjects are at that point in time. It doesn't necessarily mean that they are really weak in these. It might be that they are not quite as good at them as they are in their other subjects. It could be that they don't like them as much. I then get them to prioritise work in these subjects between now and our next meeting. When they have homework in these subjects, I recommend that they do it first, ahead of stronger or more favoured subjects. And, when they are allocating time for study and revision, to set time aside for the 'weaker' subjects first. I make it very clear to them that they must not neglect their other subjects when they are doing this.

The objective is simply to bring the 'weaker' subjects up to speed. At our next meeting, we would review the situation again. It might be that the same subjects are nominated. If so, the same approach is adopted in relation to these moving forward. If new subjects are nominated, priority is given to these in the same way until the next meeting. I believe that, with the right approach, students can become a little stronger in their 'weaker' subjects and perform better in exams as a result.

The sixth counting subject in relation to points may turn out to be the most important subject of all. It could be the one that brings you over the line for the course you really want. This is an example of why we need to become as strong as we can at our 'weaker' subjects.

All of us have weaknesses in our 'make-up'. Again, it is a matter of identifying what they are and accepting that they are inhibiting our progress. A lot of them can be as a result of bad habits being formed. A big one that springs to mind is work ethic. To succeed in school, you must be prepared to put in the required level of work. Parents constantly ask me how much should their son/daughter be doing each evening/night on homework/study/revision. My initial response is always that it is more about the quality of the work rather than the quantity.

Having said that, there is a minimum amount that I think must be done in each year. When pressed, I come up with the following:

- First-Year students: 1.5 hours daily
- Second-Year students: 2 hours daily
- Third-Year students: 3 hours daily
- Fifth-Year students: 3 hours daily
- Sixth-Year students: 4 hours daily

This must be done seven days a week.

A definite timetable is drawn up to suit each student. More about this in Chapter 5. The reason I mention it here is because I see a lack of commitment to work as the most common weakness in students. Many students struggle with applying themselves to the school-related work that must be done on a daily basis. Every student I work with on a one-to-one basis has a definite timetable for doing their homework, study and revision. They follow a really rigid timetable in school. It doesn't change. They have to adapt to it. I believe that students feel comfortable with this structure once they adapt. The same applies to doing school-related work at home.

I would first of all find out what other activities they are involved in outside of school. Also, what family commitments they have. We would then work around these and come up with a daily timetable for doing their school-related work. Once they get used to it, it becomes part of their set-up. I totally believe in this approach. It is the best way to overcome a weakness in relation to work ethic. Other weaknesses might be poor concentration, bad handwriting, not being punctual, being disorganised and being careless – to mention but a few. Once identified and, with determination, we can become stronger in areas where we have been weak. It can take time for improvement to take place. I believe that former weaknesses can eventually become strengths if we have the mindset to make that happen.

> **Note:** I have a theory about your most important subject for the Leaving Certificate being the sixth counting one in relation to points. It could be the one that brings you over the line to get that place you are looking for in university. Hence, the importance of bringing 'weaker' subjects up to speed.

Confidence

Real confidence comes from hard work and everything else that goes into preparing well. It is a combination of a lot of things. The legendary golfer, Gary Player, once said: 'The more I practice, the luckier I become.' In my opinion, it is not about luck. **The more work you put into something, the stronger you become**. The likelihood of you succeeding increases. This applies to school-related matters as well. Confidence has to be earned. It can be a slow process and it builds gradually.

Attitude has a lot to do with it. You must really want something for you to be prepared to put the required amount of work in. In the early years of secondary school, students need a lot of guidance and support in relation to this. Teachers play a big part while the students are in school. Most of their work is done with the students in groups. Parents have a role to play as well. They are in a stronger position in this regard as they can work with their son/daughter on a one-to-one basis.

It is really important that students form good habits early. **Having a good set-up for doing homework must start early in First Year**. The students are used to a rigid timetable in school. I believe they must have the same kind of set-up at home for doing their school-related work. I go through this in detail in another part of this book. I recommend three 30-minute periods per day for doing homework, study and revision for First-Year students. There should be definite times for this which can work around other activities, meal times etc.

I believe that all students are more comfortable with good structure in place. It can be difficult at the start while they get used to it. Starting off in secondary school can be really difficult as they try to get used to a totally new set-up. After a while, they just follow the timetable without thinking about it. A much simpler set up is required at home. After a while, they will get used to it. They will see that they can still be involved in all their chosen activities, have time for play, have time with their family, etc and still allocate the required time for homework, study and revision. This will develop their confidence. As they get into a really good routine, their confidence will grow. They will begin to perform well in class tests which will show them that the set-up they have in place is working. They will trust it more as time goes on and will be prepared to commit to it on an ongoing basis.

> **Note:** Real confidence comes by having good structure, trusting it and committing to it.

Coping with Set-backs

When I start working with a new student, we talk about what we are going to achieve by the end of that year. In relation to Sixth-Year students, one of the first things we do is set targeted grades for the Leaving Certificate. We will be aiming at a specific total of points. I would make it very clear that this is an outcome we are going to make happen. I would persuade the student to be very definite about this. It is not just that we would like it to happen or we hope it will happen. It is much more definite than that. *We are going to make this happen.* We establish a real determination from the start to do whatever we can to achieve the targeted points. Nothing is going to come in our way that will prevent us from achieving our goal.

This brings us back again to the importance of having a positive attitude. No matter what obstacles are put in our way, we are going to deal with them. No matter how difficult a situation might be, we will find a way to sort it. I often tell students about the following two very difficult situations that students found themselves in at crucial stages in Sixth year:

Example 1: The Lost Notes

Susan was a Sixth-Year student. In early January, she came into me for a regular meeting. She was very upset and I asked her what was causing this. She said she had left her entire set of French notes on the Dart a few days previously and that all efforts to get them back had failed.

We made one more call to Iarnród Éireann but they still hadn't turned up. I told Susan that we would find a way to deal with this serious situation. She was a top-class student looking for very high points with a specific university course in mind. French had always been her strongest and favourite subject. She was really down at that moment and believed that she would fail French as a result of what happened.

She had put a huge amount into compiling her notes and they were very important to her. I was very sympathetic with her and assured her that we would find a way to overcome this. I don't think she believed that this obstacle could be overcome at the time. I reminded her of what I had said at our first meeting at the beginning of the year: that she was going to succeed **no matter what came in her way to potentially throw her off course**. I said I would give it some thought and that I would call that night to talk about possible ways to deal with it.

We continued on with our meeting even though her morale was really low. As promised, I called her that night and told her I had a possible solution. I asked her if she had any close friends in her French class who were equally as competent as she was in the language. She said that there was one particular girl who she was close friends with and who was really good at French. I told Susan to call her to see could she borrow this girl's notes the following weekend. She was then to spend the whole weekend writing up her friend's notes and during part of the next weekend if there were still more to do. Susan wasn't totally convinced initially but was prepared to go along with my plan. She asked me about her other work. I told her we would put a plan in place to do the necessary catch-up once this problem had been solved.

She spent all of the following weekend putting a new set of French notes together. She also had to spend some of the following weekend completing the job. Once it was done, we put a plan in place to attend to the work she had sacrificed to compile the notes. Within a few weeks, everything was back to normal and she was ready to face the Mocks. I knew from that moment on that Susan would deal with everything she would face through the rest of Sixth Year and beyond. She went on to achieve her targeted points including a top grade in French.

Example 2: A Tough Start

This situation happened on the night of the opening ceremony for the European Soccer Championships. It was a Friday night and students had just completed the third day of the Leaving Certificate examinations. I was just settling down to watch the football when my mobile rang at about 7.00 p.m. It was the mother of Michael, a student I had been working with. She sounded distressed and told me he was lying on his bed feeling very down. He told her that a couple of the papers had gone badly for him and he feared the worst. He was aiming for very high points and had a specific university course in mind.

His mother went on to say that he had planned to do some revision that night for the exams that were on the next Monday but said that there was no point now. I was taken by surprise as Michael was one of my best students that year with a great work ethic. I asked her to bring him up to me immediately so I could have a chat with him.

He arrived shortly afterwards looking very deflated. I asked him to tell me what the problem was. He spent about 20 minutes filling me in on how Paper 1 in both Higher Level English and Maths hadn't gone to plan. When he finished, I told him that there was nothing he could do about those so he must focus on what was ahead. I added that they may not have been as bad as he thought. I also pointed out to him that he was doing an extra subject so he had something to fall back on in a situation like this.

I had worked on a revision plan with him for during the Leaving Certificate examinations. I knew he was due to do some revision that night, more on Saturday and Sunday with plenty of rest and recovery time built in. I also knew that he had a girlfriend who was a very positive influence on him. I told him to shut out of his mind what had happened and to focus on the revision plan for the exams on Monday. I told him to postpone the revision planned for that night, to call his girlfriend and arrange to see her for a chat and catch-up.

We added some extra time to the revision plan for the weekend and I told him to commit to it in a positive frame of mind. As it turned out, the two papers on Monday were the second ones in English and Maths. I told him to call me on Monday evening with an update on how the day had gone. He did that and was much more upbeat. The old Michael was back. The papers had gone well that day and he was back on course. The rest of the exams went really well for him and, needless to say, he achieved his targeted points.

> **Note:** Every set-back can be overcome if you have the mindset to do it.

Monitoring Progress

We have already discussed the importance of planning well. When you have what you think are the best plans in place, you must trust them and commit totally to them. Then you must monitor progress on an ongoing basis to make sure the plans are working. The student is the best judge of how things are going. Do you feel that the quality of your work is the best it can be on a consistent basis? Are you always getting all your homework done for the next day? Have you got enough time to do regular study and revision? Keep an eye on results in class tests. Also, listen to what your teachers and parents are saying. Don't be afraid to take on board constructive criticism from those who know and care. They may be able to point something out to you that will make a difference. Make sure that you have adequate breaks built into your set-up. Do you find that you are too tired when facing into a late session?

There is no point in persisting with something that is not working. Heed the warning signs and take action. You might have to re-schedule that session for an earlier time on another day. It can take a bit of tinkering with in the early stages before you get it right. A lot of thought and effort must go in at the planning stage before you get the best set-up for you. Don't be afraid to change something that is not working. Review your set-up on a regular basis. I have this on the agenda of every meeting with the students I work with.

Circumstances can change so adjustments have to be made in your set-up to reflect these. Some extra-curricular activities students get involved in are seasonal. Changes may need to be made as a result of these. Where possible, you should not alter the set-up too much. Students become used to a set routine and change can sometimes disrupt their performance. Only make changes where you have to and where they will improve the overall set-up. Monitoring progress is a good way of gauging how your set-up is working.

> **Note:** Be decisive in making a change to your set-up if an aspect of it is not working.

Attendance and Punctuality

Every student should aim to have full attendance at school. Absences should be kept to a minimum. Regular absences can totally disrupt progress. I have seen situations where students fail to recover from what they missed out on through being absent. A student should only be absent when it is totally unavoidable. When this happens, a student must make sure that they are not going to be at a disadvantage because of the time missed. They must be pro-active in this regard. They must find out what they missed in each subject while they were out. This can be done through direct contact with subject teachers. I encourage students I work with to build up a network of friends with this in mind. If you have at least one friend in each subject, you can make sure to find out what you missed and address the necessary catch-up work involved. You can do the same for friends when they are absent. You have to take responsibility here. You have to be determined that you are not going to miss out because you couldn't avoid being absent. Don't wait for the information to come to you. You have to go looking for it.

> **Note:** The aim at the start of each school year should be to achieve full attendance.

I am a real stickler for punctuality. I put a big emphasis on being on time. If you are going to perfect time management for your exams, you must work on it in your everyday life. If you are a little careless about it on a day-to-day basis, you will be the same when it comes to exams.

It starts with being on time for school every morning. Then, be on time for each class period throughout the day. Be on time for your supervised study. The biggest test is in relation to your timetable for sessions at home. You must be really disciplined here. You must be ready to start each session at the appointed time. Being punctual will then become part of your life. It is all part of forming good habits. The time management side of examinations will be much easier to perfect if you are conscious of it in your everyday life.

> **Note:** Being on time is something you can control if you have the mindset to do it.

Chapter 9

Other Aspects to Consider

'Work in Progress' Notebook

A few years ago, a student I was working with told me that his head was full of work that he had to do. He said that it was distracting him when he was trying to focus on the work he was doing. I told him that he needed to park it somewhere and totally shut it out of his mind. I recommended listing such work in a notebook. I decided to call it a 'work in progress' notebook. I told him to list in it **all the important work that he had to do but just couldn't get to right now.** I said that he should include difficulties/problems he encounters which have to be addressed. He should then prioritise and deal with each item in order of importance/urgency. When he has spare time available, he should select from the list and tick it off when done. It then becomes an ongoing process.

All the students I have worked with on one to one over the past few years have used it. I have received very positive feedback on the benefit they derive from using it. They find that their minds are less cluttered which leads to better quality focus and concentration. My feeling is that it brings a little more structure to their set-up.

For this to work well, there must be good discipline. They must check the notebook regularly to see to see what has to be done. They must allocate time to deal with the items on the list. One girl said recently that the list was growing and she just wasn't getting to deal with this work. She was a little concerned about this. We had to add a little time to her weekly work schedules to enable her to deal with this. Soon, she was making in-roads into the list. Weekends and mid-terms/holidays create good opportunities to address such work. It is not just about the notebook here. It is more about the actual concept. One of my students doesn't use a specific notebook but uses a combination of a white board, her phone and her school journal.

> **Note:** The simple process of listing work to be done in a notebook can take a weight off your mind.

Examinations Notebook

I have a very definite view on how to approach tests/house examinations on the way to the Leaving Certificate examination itself. Most people would say that the most important thing about a test/house exam is the result. Yes, the result is important, but it is more about gaining experience for doing the Leaving Certificate itself. I would have the same approach in relation to the Junior Certificate examinations. In relation to the Leaving Certificate, I am focusing on Fifth and Sixth Year, a two-year cycle.

I have introduced what I call an examinations notebook for Leaving Certificate students I am working with one to one. The purpose of it is **to help each student gain maximum benefit from doing tests and examinations on the way to the Leaving Certificate itself**. The latter is all about the results and the points achieved. We can't get away from that.

There are three aspects to the examinations notebook. Say for example you are having an English test involving writing an essay. The first aspect is to record how your preparations went for the test. In particular, the student will write in details of what didn't go particularly well in the preparations. Then, the second aspect has to do with writing in brief details of how the test went. In particular, anything that didn't go well. It might be that I ran out of time at the end and was rushing to finish it. And, finally, the third aspect has to do with the returned script. Go through it in detail to identify where you lost marks. Then, do whatever follow-up work necessary so that the same mistakes won't be made again.

If a student of mine gets 81% in a test, I want to know about the 19%. Yes, the student deserves credit for getting a top mark. I accept that. I want them to get top marks in the Leaving Certificate. As a result, I want them to learn all they can from tests, etc along the way. My objective at the end of each process following a test is that they would get 100% in it if they resat it. My theory is that every student should be stronger as a result of doing a test and using the examinations notebook process as well. I would put a big emphasis on using this process for the summer exams at the end of Fifth Year and for the Mock examinations in Sixth Year. Students could be doing follow-up work on the Mocks up until May. It is an ongoing process and must be completed. In some schools, Sixth Year students do Christmas exams as well in late November/early December. The examinations notebook would be used for these as well. There is a discipline involved around the process of doing tests/house examinations that is geared towards each student gaining maximum benefit from the experience of doing them.

> **Note:** If we are to perform to our ability in the Leaving Certificate, we must gain maximum benefit from all experiences along the way. Tests and house examinations are an important part of that. Using the examinations notebook will enable us to do this.

'Add-Value' Theory

As far as I am concerned, work should never be done just for the sake of doing it. There always should be a good reason for doing the work you have chosen. In relation to homework, it is straightforward. Subject teachers prescribe work to be done and set deadlines for it to be submitted. A lot of the time, students get it done as quickly as possible just because it has to be done. I can understand their thinking, but a more positive attitude is required. I want each student to be better off following work being done, including homework. The emphasis must always be on making all work undertaken the best it can possibly be.

It is important to take a real pride in all work you do. On completing each item of work, you must be stronger as a result of doing it.

Along with homework, I am referring to work done in class at school, revision and study done at supervised study in school and at home, doing questions from past papers, preparing notes, doing follow-up work following class tests, doing additional work on areas where you were having difficulty, and so on. The 'work in progress' notebook is a great way to record, organise and control all work to be done. I sometimes ask students to grade themselves on the quality of work done in a session. If a student is looking for a H1 in a subject in the Leaving Cert, the quality of the work should be consistently of a H1 standard. For me, the priority should always be to make each item of work done the best it can possibly be.

Approach to Class Tests

Students should benefit from each class test taken. I am more inter-ested in the marks lost rather than the marks gained. If a student gets 80% in a class test, I am more interested in the 20% lost. They must identify why the marks were lost and what follow-up work needs to be done to make sure that similar marks won't be lost in a future class test. The follow-up work should then be listed in the 'work in progress' notebook and done when time becomes available.

It must be remembered that class tests are part of the preparation for Junior and Leaving Certificate examinations. Every student wants to do their best in class tests and it is great when this happens. Where they don't, it is important to identify why and address the issue. The most common reason is lack of preparation/work. As mentioned, this can be addressed by doing the follow-up work.

Another cause might be to do with time management issues. This can be addressed by practicing similar questions under test condi-tions and being disciplined with regard to completing answers within the stipulated time.

Sometimes it can be to do with misinterpreting what the question is asking and not providing the content that is sought. This is all part of developing good exam technique. This is covered in Chapter 7. It is one thing knowing the subject material really well. It is another skill coming up with suitable responses under exam conditions.

'Weaker' Areas in Our Make-Up

As far as I am concerned, a big emphasis must always be put on making 'weaker' elements in our make-up as strong as they possibly can be. As a rugby coach, for the most part, I agreed with the approach to always play to your strengths. However, a big priority for me was to focus on 'weaker' members of the squad and doing what was required to make them as good as they could be. I agree with the saying 'a team is as strong as its weakest link'. Most times, this just meant working harder at the 'weaker' elements of each individual's game. I would arrange extra training sessions to address this.

The same applies for students preparing for examinations. There can be a tendency to neglect 'weaker' or less favoured subjects. This can also apply to something in your make-up or in the way you do things. A weakness must be identified first of all and then a way must be found to sort it. There is no point in continuing with something that is not working. We must continually review how our overall plan is working and make changes where necessary. A plan that was perfect three months ago may not be now. Circumstances change so we must adjust our plan accordingly. Students often say to me that they can struggle with a session late at night. They may have had a particularly demanding day leading to tiredness setting in earlier than normal. In such a situation, it is fine to re-schedule that session. There always has to be a degree of flexibility built into every plan to cater for such an eventuality.

I have a theory about a Leaving Cert student's most important subject. For me, it is the sixth one counting for points. I maintain that students will maximise their overall points if they get this subject to its targeted grade level. We can sometimes accept weaknesses we have and do nothing about them. I am not saying that we can become really strong in areas where we are weak. However, what I am saying is that we can always become a little stronger in weaker areas with increased effort and determination, which can make a big difference. Results can be decided on small margins so we must be as strong as possible in every area/subject.

Dealing with Problems and Difficulties

Many students can struggle because they don't deal with problems/difficulties as they arise. Students must be decisive here. Once a problem or difficulty is identified, a way of dealing with it must be found. I ask students I work with to let me know when they are faced with such a problem or difficulty. I get them to use the 'work in progress' notebook for recording it. The fact that it is now listed with things to be done means it won't be forgotten. There might be a very simple solution to sorting it out. It might simply require a little additional work to sort it. It might need some research to get to the bottom of it.

Students nowadays are very fortunate in that all information is available to them if they want to access it. Information and help are available online 24/7. In some cases, a student may need help to sort out a problem or difficulty. I always say to students that they should build up a network of friends to consult. If possible, it would be good to have at least one friend in each subject who could be contacted if such a situation arises. It works both ways. They can contact you if they are trying to sort out a problem or difficulty. It may require the student contacting their subject teacher to solve the issue. I always say to Leaving Certificate students that they will be able to sort out most problems/difficulties themselves if they have a mindset to do it. The important thing is that a way must be found to sort it.

A lot of the time, when a problem or difficulty arises, the solution is very simple. The person sitting beside you might be able to sort it. Never be afraid to admit that you are struggling with something. Sharing your predicament can help a lot. If you are just not getting to the bottom of something, let your Mum and Dad know. They may be able to advise you on how to solve it. You may have to go to your subject teacher. Whatever it takes, be determined to do it.

Note: Ignoring a difficulty or problem will hold up progress. A solution must be found as a matter of urgency so that you can move on.

Having a Healthy Lifestyle

It is really important that each student remains as healthy as possible throughout the year. There will be times when they may have to miss time at school through illness. Then, every effort must be made to ensure that the student makes up for the lost time and is not at a disadvantage overall.

A healthy lifestyle will minimise the amount of disruption through illness. A big part of this is having a healthy diet. Consuming healthy food and drinks on a daily basis will play a big part in making sure that each student stays fit and well. Having the right amount of physical exercise is also important. This is where participating in sporting activities is great. Students get the exercise they need while playing the sport they love. Where a student is not into sport, just getting out for a good walk can be just as good. As I said earlier, it is so important to get the balance right between school work and leisure activities. The planning of the latter is just as important as the homework, study and revision. It is all about getting the balance right.

Dehydration can be a problem for students. I particularly think of examinations time at the beginning of the summer. It is so important to stay hydrated. A bottle of still water is one of the most important items to have with you as an accessory. This applies at all times of the year as well. We must do whatever it takes to keep our energy levels up at all times. This is where the right type of food at the right times is essential. What I bring with me for lunch each day is really important. It is crucial at key times when I am working really hard. What I eat at break times during my work schedule is critical. It is so important to have high energy levels when it matters. I think of important matches in sport. I think of examination time for students. However, it is all about having a balanced diet and exercise regime on a daily basis and ensuring this becomes a permanent part of our lifestyle.

Chapter 10

Getting the Balance Right in Your Life

Too much of anything is not good. A lot of students tend to cram work as the Leaving Certificate approaches. The only reason for this is because the work wasn't done on a consistent basis through the year.

I was working with a student two years ago who was involved in sport at an elite level. For about half of Sixth Year, he wasn't able to give the time required to his school work. He told me that once his commitment to his sport was over (to be around the middle of March), he said that he would give all of his time to his studies from then until the end of the Leaving Certificate examinations. He was looking for high points so there was a lot to do.

I knew that his plan to commit totally to his studies to the exclusion of everything else just wouldn't work. For a start, his body was used to a lot of regular physical activity. The change he was proposing was too drastic. When his serious involvement in sport was at an end for that year, I sat down with him to put a plan in place. I told him that it would be essential to have certain amount of physical activity in his life moving forward. We arranged that he would do five workouts in the gym a week. He told me that there was an indoor soccer tournament taking place in the school from then until the start of May. I told him to put his name down for that. I also convinced him that regular walks listening to his music (he told me before that he found listening to music very relaxing) would be a good idea. Anyway, between all of these activities, I knew we would have the balance required. We then set about drawing up his homework, study and revision sessions for the week. We included enough to get him back on track to achieve his targeted grades. Even though he had a lot of catch up work to do, I knew there had to be really good balance if the plan was to work. Also, it was essential that he still had adequate physical activity in his daily routine. Going from one extreme to another just wouldn't have worked.

I am a great believer in sticking with a routine you are comfortable with. Having good balance is a very important part of this. Students can fall into the trap of trying to change too much as the Leaving Certificate gets closer. Good balance probably becomes even more important as the examinations approach. As much as possible, continue with the leisure activities that you really enjoy and that are good for your overall wellbeing. All of this is possible with good planning. I would go so far as to say it is essential if the quality of your school-related work is to be at the desired levels. It is all part of staying in control as the time nears. Focus on the process and let the results take care of themselves. It is all about pacing yourself through the year. The objective is to have you in the form of your life for the duration of the Leaving Certificate examinations. You don't want to be too tired on the examination days because of too much cramming in the lead up to them.

Early-morning Work/Late-night Work

A lot of people say that very early in the morning is the best time to study. I don't disagree with this but it is not for everybody. Some students are 'morning people'. They have no problem getting up really early and can get really good work done even before school starts. I was never one of these. During my university years, I tried getting up really early to do study/revision before lectures started. I always felt that I was too tired this early to get any quality work done and, worst of all, I became really tired early in the evening because of being up so early. I always talk to my students about this when we are planning the year ahead. One of my students this year was a real 'morning person'. He was very comfortable with getting up before 6.00 a.m. each morning, doing a workout in the gym and getting an hour's study/revision done before school started. This became part of his plan. We had to make sure that he got to bed early enough in the evening so as to get the required number of hours' sleep. Something like this just wouldn't have worked for most of my students. It comes down to individual preferences. You don't have something in your plan that is not going to work for you.

In relation to late-night work, small breaks in between sessions can help with your stamina. A little bit of fresh air before that last session can give you a second wind. You don't want to be working too late at night either. A student might come to me and say the last session on a Thursday night (say 9.40 to 10 p.m.) is a waste of time. They might say to me that they are just too tired because it is so late in the week. I would say that there is no point in persisting with it if it is not working. It is all about the quality of work. If they can tell me that homework is normally done at this stage, I would suggest that they drop this one and do an extra one at the weekend. We have to find a way to make sure that the quality of work in all sessions is of the required standard on a consistent basis. It might take a bit of time at the beginning of the year to get the overall plan the best it can be. It can be a bit of trial and error during the first few weeks. Eventually, you will arrive at the plan that suits you best.

Cramming Work in Close to the Leaving Certificate Examinations

I would never say to a student that they shouldn't cram work in at the end. If important work hasn't been done at that stage, it must be done. It is not a great way to put together your final preparations but needs must. It means that your overall plan hasn't worked. I have spoken before about the importance of planning well so that late cramming won't be needed. There should be no need for a lot of heavy work immediately before the start of the Leaving Certificate examinations. All of this should have been already done.

A big emphasis in the overall plan should be on consistency of work over the whole year. At the end, it should all be light revision from specially-prepared notes and sample answers to examination questions. There is nothing wrong with having to do some extra work in key areas. If there is too much to be done, it can lead to panic at the end and the student not being in the right frame of mind to perform well. In my opinion, students who have to cram a lot in at the end don't achieve results they are capable of getting. It turns out to be a battle and a struggle for them. They are not really in control and it can be down to damages limitations. They will achieve 'OK' results but not what they should have got. It comes down to them not applying themselves consistently to the overall plan from the start.

Grinds

I am in favour of grinds only if they are used in the right way. The primary source of information and tuition is in your school. If your attitude is right, you will get all you need from your teachers in each subject. You then back this up by fulfilling your part of the bargain. This involves doing the required amount of work on a consistent basis and dealing with any problems/difficulties that arise. All of this is covered at different stages throughout the book.

Where a student is struggling in a particular subject, additional help may be required. My view is that the student should continue to work as hard as possible and be totally positive about gaining maximum benefit from attendance at class in that subject. Grinds may then be necessary as well. The student must have the right approach to grinds. They should look on them as supplementary help. The grinds should focus on the key areas where the student is having difficulty. They should do follow-up work on the material covered in each session and prepare their own notes. They should do this even where they are given handouts. I am a great believer in this process of making your own notes. Also, the student should bring to the attention of the tutor aspects where they are struggling. They must be proactive in what is going on and make sure that the work that is being done is exactly what is required.

Some students attend classes in grind schools during their mid-terms/breaks. Again, this is fine if done for the right reasons. There are some very good revision courses in all subjects. Again, they must be done for the right reasons and appropriate follow-up work should take place following them. All of this should be supplementary to the main work.

Chapter 11

Coping in a Crisis – the Coronavirus Pandemic

One of the first things I say to a student is that they are going to succeed no matter what they are faced with. I never thought in my wildest dreams that they would have to face anything like the Covid-19 pandemic. It is amazing how resilient students can be when they put their minds to it. It is all about being really determined to sort any obstacle they are confronted with.

Dealing with Whatever We Are Faced With

The coronavirus crisis appeared with very little warning. One minute, life was going on very much as normal, the next minute we were in the middle of a crisis the likes of which was never seen before. We were suddenly facing into totally unprecedented times. Every aspect of life was going to be affected by what was happening. Scientists and health experts were going to determine how our lives would change dramatically in a very short period of time. One of the first big changes announced was that schools and colleges were to close, initially for a period of two to three weeks. The decision caught a lot of people by surprise and schools had very little time to prepare teachers and students for what was about to happen. The attitude had to be 'let's do the best we can with what we are now faced with'.

The Importance of Structure

The first thing that came into my mind was the importance of structure. Under normal circumstances, structure and routine are essential. Under totally abnormal circumstances, they assume an even greater importance. We were about to embark on a journey into the unknown. Students, I felt, would need a strong element of structure in their lives to enable them to survive through the tough times that lay ahead. A big consideration at the time was the uncertainty of what was happening and lack of clarity with regard to the future. My advice to students at that time was to accept what was happening and not to look too far ahead. I also advised them not to listen to rumours, speculation, false news, etc. and only to follow official news bulletins. The decision to close schools would bring us up to the Easter break. I impressed upon students not to look beyond this at that point.

Schools informed their students that there would be ongoing communication with them remotely. It became apparent very quickly that there would be difficulty implementing this. Some teachers lacked the experience/expertise in digital technology to be able to deliver in relation to all of this. Also, certain homes did not have access to online communication. As far as possible, schools were going to operate their normal daily timetables so students were to do the same at home. This all sounded great in theory but difficult to make happen. I felt it was the right approach to take by schools but that there had to be a large degree of flexibility built in. What they were trying to do would bring a large degree of structure to the set-up, which was what was needed. As it turned out, some of it worked really well and some not so well. My advice to the students I was working with was to adhere to the daily school timetable and be available for when classes were going to be delivered remotely. However, I impressed upon them the importance of having a Plan B if certain class periods didn't happen. Students told me that when they logged in for a remote lesson they were informed about, sometimes there was nothing there. In that event, my advice was to have work ready to do if it didn't happen. It became very clear that teachers were finding their way as much as students. Part of the new set-up involved teachers giving homework to be done with deadlines for it to be submitted for correction. The feedback on the work wasn't always forthcoming. I advised my students to be proactive in seeking this feedback by way of reminders emailed to subject teachers. Every effort was being made on behalf of schools to make the new set-up work but, understandably, there were difficulties which required a lot of patience from everyone.

Balance between School-related Work and Leisure/Exercise/Rest and Recovery Time

Under normal circumstances, I put a huge emphasis on the balance between school-related work and leisure/exercise/rest and recovery time. During the extraordinary times of the coronavirus pandemic, the time spent away from homework, study and revision becomes even more important. Because of the restrictions that were in place by way of social distancing and limited movement, a lot of attention was required with regard to coming up with a daily routine for leisure/exercise/rest and recovery. I suggested to students that they would have to use their imagination a lot to come up with adequate activities. The normal activities they were involved in may not have been possible because of the circumstances they were faced with. I felt it was essential for them to bring real structure to these leisure activities as well.

I recommended that they included as much physical activity as possible. As they were going to follow the normal school timetable on a daily basis, they would have to work around this. I suggested doing one of the Joe Wicks exercise routines available on YouTube early each morning, fit in a walk/run during the day when the timetable would permit and maybe some circuit training in between when the school timetable finishes and doing additional homework, etc. later. My advice was that this should be planned in advance just like with the school-related work. Plenty of thought had to go into it to come up with the overall plan that would work for each student.

Additional Pressure Experienced in a Crisis

I mentioned already that teachers were finding it difficult adapting to teaching remotely. Also, the feedback I was getting was that they were finding each day tougher and more demanding than a normal school day would be. The same was happening with the students. With them, they were worried about the uncertainty of it all. Would the Junior and Leaving Certificate examinations be going ahead in June was the question foremost on their minds. My advice to them at the time was to shut this uncertainty out of their minds and to focus totally on what they had to do. The word from the Department of Education was that they were going ahead in June so I impressed upon them the importance of preparing for that to happen.

What struck me at the time was that each school was providing a service remotely on a daily basis using their normal timetable and that students needed to embrace this. Yes, there were difficulties on both sides but the overall set-up would improve in time if everyone bought into it. Students needed to commit to it and make the best of what was being provided. These were very difficult times which required the cooperation of all concerned.

I could see that the period following the closedown of the schools was taking its toll on teachers and students alike. The morale among the students I was working with was low as we approached the Easter break. I knew that they needed a change for the two weeks of the break with a lot of leisure/rest and recovery time built in. Schools for the most part wouldn't be providing remote services during this time. I recommended my normal Easter break routine to my students with just school-related work on eight of the sixteen days. I felt that this would strike the right balance, giving them much needed rest time along with quality work time with the exams still scheduled for June.

Junior Certificate Examinations Cancelled

On Good Friday (10 April 2020), the Minister for Education announced that the Junior Certificate examinations were being cancelled and the Leaving Certificate examinations were being pushed back to start on Wednesday 29 July.

With regard to Third-Year students, the word from the Department of Education was that schools would be holding in-house exams in all subjects early in the school year 2020/2021. My immediate advice for the students I was working with was to look on these as their official Junior Certificate exams and to prepare accordingly. I knew that a big difficulty with this was the summer holidays coming in the middle of the preparations. I told them not to look too far ahead and just to focus on what had to be done up to the end of May. After the Easter break, they resumed their remote learning and were encouraged to take each day at a time. On Friday 8 May, a further decision was made by the Department of Education abandoning the plan to hold in-house exams in September and to bring a close to the Junior Cycle at the end of May. At least this brought real clarity to what was happening, and the students knew that they didn't have to look beyond the current school year.

The end-of-year report would be based on a number of things – results in exams/tests already held, performance in class/remote learning and remote exams to be held at the end of May. They could do nothing now about exams/tests already held and performance in class before the school closed. They just had to focus on performance in remote learning from then on and preparing as best they could for the remote exams at the end of May. I made it very clear to them that the summer report was now going to be their official Junior Certificate results.

Leaving Certificate Examinations Pushed Back

With regard to Sixth-Year students, once the decision was made to push the Leaving Certificate Exams back to start on 29 July, I told the students I was working with to take the second week of the Easter break totally off. They had an extra two months to prepare so they needed some quality time off to reflect and get into a positive frame of mind about what lay ahead. I encouraged them to look on it as an opportunity to prepare even better and to take full advantage of the additional time available. The initial reaction from most of them was one of disappointment. All they could see was that it was now going to totally disrupt their summer and that peaking in June was not now the objective.

Once the students got over the initial disappointment, they eventually came around to see that they could turn this new situation to their advantage. It now meant planning differently to take the new circumstances into consideration. Once the students accepted what was happening, they were then able to get back to serious preparation and take full advantage of the additional time. A big distraction for them at the time was all the speculation in the media about what may happen and the possibility of the Leaving Certificate exams not taking place at all. My advice to them was to only listen to the official word from the Department of Education, which at the time was that the exams would be taking place in late July/August. They had no other option but to keep preparing for this. Still, it was very difficult for them to ignore the increased level of coverage in the media. Finally, on Friday 8 May, the Minister for Education announced that the exams were being cancelled and were being replaced by a system of 'calculated grades'. Students would also have the option of sitting exams later in the year.

Calculated Grades

My main concern about 'calculated grades' was that the system may not be fair to the students. They experienced a huge amount of disruption through the Covid-19 pandemic so the least they deserved was to be treated fairly with this grading system. We don't have a culture of calculated or predicted grades at Leaving Certificate level. Teachers would feel uncomfortable with it and would need a lot of support and guidance in relation to how to administer it. It is one thing if you know in advance that it is going to be used. Trying to do it retrospectively is much more difficult.

In my view, it should include an element of predictive grading as well. Students would have made a lot of progress since sitting Christmas and Mock exams. They will have learned a lot from the experience of sitting the Mock exams in particular. I always kept a record of students' Mock results and then compared them with the actual results in the Leaving Cert. Over a fifteen-year period, on average, results were always 20% higher in the Leaving Cert. I once had a student who failed his Mock but got the top grade in Higher-Level Accounting in the actual exam. It has to be about predicting what each student would have got rather than what was historically achieved in tests/exams in the past. This would not be easy to do but a way had to be found, otherwise we would be letting the class of 2020 down.

School Year 2020/2021

Once the decision was taken for schools to open fully at the start of academic year 2020/2021, the health and safety of staff and students was the absolute priority. Senior management, along with other members of staff, in all schools spent most of the summer getting everything ready. Very strict guidelines were provided by the Department of Education. Life in school was going to be very different. Masks would have to be worn at all times by staff and students. There would be restricted movement during the school day. Year groups would be confined to certain areas to minimize movement. Desktops would have to be sanitised after each period and so on. A huge amount of time, effort and resources were being put into providing as safe an environment as possible for school life to continue. Substantial financial aid was being provided for all schools to cover the additional expenditure incurred.

With regard to teaching and learning, it appeared to me that the emphasis was being diverted away from it a little because of the impact of Covid. This was likely to continue for some considerable time. There was an even greater need for students to take more responsibility for their own learning. Some schools weren't going to be able to offer the same supervised study facilities that had been available before the pandemic came. This meant that more time at home would have to be included in the overall plan for doing homework, study and revision. One of the biggest changes that lasted all the way through school year 2020/21 was in relation to team sports, which just didn't happen. My advice for students was to come up with other activities where social distancing guidelines could be adhered to. Team sports needed to be replaced with physical exercise that could be undertaken. If it had to be done on an individual basis, so be it. Running or walking, doing exercise or circuit training, setting up skills drills for a particular sport are all activities that could be undertaken while adhering to social distancing protocols. I recommended to students to use their imaginations to come up with physical activities to undertake. It was more important than ever that the right balance between work and leisure was maintained.

The Leaving Cert class of 2021 had to endure two periods of lockdown, one while in Fifth Year and the other while in Sixth Year. The

Department of Education put in place a system of accredited grades as well as the Leaving Certificate examinations. Every student was to get an accredited grade in each subject. Students could then sit examinations in all their subjects or just ones of their choice. In subjects where they did the exam, they would be given the better grade of the two. It seemed a very fair set-up following all they had been through during the previous two years.

School Year 2021/2022

The school year started off a lot closer to normal compared with the previous eighteen months. However, Covid-19, mainly due to the presence of the Delta variant, was still around. New cases and hospital numbers remained high, which meant that there was still a nervousness about. Certain restrictions like the wearing of masks and elements of social distancing remained in place. The hope was that the Junior and Leaving Cert exams would take place as normal in June 2022. Students had to assume this and prepare accordingly. We were still dealing with a crisis and students had to be prepared to deal with whatever they were faced with. Good planning leading to suitable structures being in place became more important than ever. A really positive note was that the playing of team sports had returned. This was a really big step forward in the journey towards normal life resuming. The hope was that the class of 2022 would have a clear run up to the Leaving Cert exams in June. The same would apply for Junior Cert students.

Even though school life was a lot closer to normal compared with the previous eighteen months, Junior and Leaving Cert students had experienced really difficult times during Second and Fifth Year. However, the Department of Education was adamant that there would be no calculated/predicted grades for Leaving Cert students. They wanted normal examinations to resume. The only concession they made was that there would be better choices in all subjects. They also said that results would be at the same level that they were at in the previous year. Because of this, it is very likely that points required for courses at third level will remain at the same high levels as occurred the previous year. My advice for the Leaving Cert students I was working with was to take nothing for granted. Consistent application to the work schedules in place for each period was required, which would give each student the best chance of realising their potential. At the time of writing, the Junior and Leaving Cert exams have been completed. Any Leaving Cert students who couldn't sit their exams in June due to Covid have been given an opportunity to re-sit them at a later date.

Learning from Living with Covid-19

Covid-19 arrived out of the blue with absolutely no warning and disrupted all our lives for more than two years. We still haven't seen the end of it and its presence continues to disrupt our lives to a certain degree. For secondary school students, it has been a huge learning curve trying to adapt to sudden changing circumstances. I often say that students have to be flexible and adaptable under normal circumstances. This took on a whole new meaning as they did their best to cope with the coronavirus pandemic. Every student will be much stronger as a result of the experience they have gained coming through it. There are always going to be obstacles/setbacks to deal with but there will never ever be one on the scale of Covid-19. Students can move forward with confidence knowing that they have come through as tough an experience as they are likely to meet and are now very well equipped to cope with whatever they have to face in the future.

Chapter 12

Conclusion

Working with My Granddaughter

I look back now on a wonderful career, the majority of it being spent in St Brendan's College, Woodbrook, Bray (now known as Woodbrook College). From the day I started there in September 1971 to do teaching practice for the Higher Diploma in Education right up to retiring as principal there in 2009, I had a brilliant time. All of the students were the 'salt of the earth'. We always had a real variety of students from highly motivated academic ones to many from disadvantaged backgrounds. There were many from middle-class backgrounds as well. It was a great place to teach as you experienced all kinds of students. I never wanted to leave the place, which remained with me right up to the end of my time there.

From a very early stage, I saw the need for one-to-one contact with students outside of their formal schooling. I felt that every student would benefit from such a service. I could see that school life in general is just too busy to even contemplate such an idea. I was determined going back over 30 years to set up a service like this. I achieved this on my retirement in 2009 when I set up my One2One mentoring service for secondary school students. I have developed it over the last thirteen years to what it is today. I get great feedback from the students I work with (and their parents) and would like to think it makes a difference in their lives. I certainly have enjoyed my involvement in it. Just as in the previous 38 years, I have met wonderful students over the last thirteen years through One2One mentoring. It has been all I thought it would be and a perfect 'next stage' in my career.

The highlight for me over the past decade has been working with my eldest grandchild, Sophie. I was very reluctant at the start to include her as one of my students as I just wanted to be her grandad. My total belief in what I was doing convinced me to include her as one of my students. I made one thing very clear to her at the start before we commenced at the beginning of her first year in secondary school. I told her that, first and foremost, she is my granddaughter and I her grandad. I said that if any of the mentoring interfered with that, we would end that side of things. Also, I said that we would start and finish each meeting with a hug. I have worked with Sophie for five years (Transition Year being the exception). I have to be honest and say that it has totally enhanced our overall relationship. I needn't have worried at all. Sophie is a wonderful girl in every way and will make a success of whatever she decides to do in life after school.

Summary of Main Aspects
Planning well

The start of every year is vital. Even more so for Junior and Leaving Certificate students. Having the best overall plan in place for the year gives each student a clear vision for what lies ahead. The uncertainty of the unknown can be daunting. Good planning can eliminate a lot of this. Once a long-term plan is in place, it is easier to focus on the short and medium-term plans. Short term for me is the day-to-day planning. A simple way of looking on this is trying to make everything you do each day the best it can be. This applies to inside and outside of School. Medium term would apply to each School Term. Plans are only effective if you commit and apply yourself to them on a consistent basis. Good planning brings real structure to everything and gives you the best chance of succeeding. A big part of this is putting the three work schedules in place for doing homework, study and revision.

Once these are in place, each student must be prepared to commit totally on a consistent basis.

Critical appraisal of where each student stands at the start of the year

There must be real honesty when doing this. It is really important that we have an accurate assessment of where the student is starting from. This would include critically appraising how they have performed academically up to this point. An examination of the most recent school report would be appropriate. Teacher comments about application and commitment in the past must be taken into consideration. What are parents saying about their son's/daughter's approach to homework, study and revision? And, most importantly, what is the student saying? Strong areas need to be identified with an emphasis on more of the same moving forward. On the other hand, weaker areas must be highlighted and ways found to address these for the future. All of this is really important preparation to make sure that the overall plan put in place for the coming year is the best one possible.

As I have mentioned earlier in the book, I always get each student to nominate their two 'weaker' subjects. This is not to say that they are weak at these. It is just pointing out that there is room for improvement. My theory is that, if we can make the two 'weaker' subjects as strong as they can possibly be, we are close to the best overall situation we can be in. The danger here is that we may neglect stronger subjects in an effort to tackle the weaker ones. This can't be allowed to happen. We can keep a close watch on this with regular monitoring of progress.

Leisure/sport/family/rest and recovery time

This area is mentioned a lot through the book as I consider it crucial in the context of the overall plan. I have been quoted as saying that it is at least as important as the school-related work and may be even more important. Too much work in my opinion is worse than too little. The optimum situation is when a good balance is achieved. Good quality leisure time makes quality work possible.

When putting the work schedules together, the leisure activities need to go in first. I love students who are busy outside of the academic side. I always try to cater for the activities a student wants to be involved in. I like to see this happening right the way through the year. Students gain comfort from consistency. In my opinion, it is wrong to change things too much when we are getting close to exams. With good planning, things can be spread out in a way that cramming can be avoided at the end.

Definite timetables for homework, study and revision

Everything in secondary school is streamlined and structured. The service is second to none. Students are then expected to organise their lives outside of school themselves. This is a difficult task even for the best of students. It is essential that real structure is introduced otherwise everything will be too loose. This is where the three schedules of work come in.

- **Schedule of work for normal school days**: This will run for the whole school year on days when normal school is on. It will work around the daily commitments each student has. There will be a recommended quantity of time each day – this will vary from an hour-and-a-half for First-Year students to four hours for Sixth-Year students. A definite daily timetable is drawn up for each individual student. It may have to be tweaked a bit over the first couple of weeks before the most suitable one is arrived at. Once this happens, the student must commit to what is in place on a consistent basis.
- **Schedule for weekends when normal school is on**: A big emphasis at weekends has to be on leisure time. Weekdays will be very demanding when normal school is on so adequate time for re-charging the batteries must be created. Again, commitments outside of school-related work go in first. Again, there will be a recommended quantity of time each weekend for school-related work – this will vary from three hours for First-Year students to eight hours for Sixth-Year students. Again, a definite timetable will be drawn up.
- **Schedules for mid-terms and holiday periods**: There are four of these in the school year – the October mid-term break, the Christmas break, the February mid-term break and the Easter

break. I go through these in detail at different stages in the book with examples. Again, there is a huge emphasis on leisure activities, etc but there are opportunities for quality school-related work to be done as well. Each break must be planned carefully in advance to achieve the right balance. I insist that much more of the time in each break is set aside for leisure activities, etc.

Breaking the year up into periods

There is a chapter devoted to this as it is a critical part of the overall plan. I break the year up into eleven periods for Junior and Leaving Certificate students. There is one less for First, Second- and Fifth-Year students. The main objective with all of this is to get each student to focus totally on the period they are in and avoid the temptation of looking too far ahead. It gets them to focus totally on the process they have in place. In my opinion, this will give them the best chance of realising their potential and achieving their targeted grades in the end-of-year examinations. My objective for each student is for them to be able to look back after the last exam and say 'I couldn't have done any more.' If they can say this, they will normally achieve their targeted grades.

The 'work in progress' notebook

I mentioned earlier in the book about the student who came to me one day and said that all the work he still had to do was dominating his thoughts and distracting him from work he was trying to do. My solution was to park things temporarily by listing them in a notebook. I called it a 'work in progress' notebook. Each student has to check it regularly, particularly when they have time available to do extra work. They need to prioritise in relation to what is in it and address more urgent items first. I also tell them that they need to be patient and that they will get around to dealing with everything in time. The student that came to me in the first place said that it made a huge difference to him moving forward and was instrumental in him achieving his goals. That was a few years ago now. Since then, every student I have worked with has used it and they have found it to be a great help. It is another example to me of how important it is to look after the little things.

The examinations notebook

I wanted to find a way where students can get the most out of house examinations and class tests that they do. The Mock exams for Third- and Sixth-Year students spring to mind. These are practice runs for the Junior and Leaving Certificate students. The main objective is to learn as much as they can from the experience of doing them. That is why I introduced the examinations notebook and I outline how it works in an earlier section in the book. I also want each student to apply the concept when doing class tests, etc. In simple terms, they must identify where there was a weakness and then do the necessary follow-up work to address it. It is all about being stronger as a result of everything we go through and always learning from our mistakes – making sure we won't make the same mistake again.

Dealing with problems/difficulties and coping with setbacks

Students are always going to have problems/difficulties to deal with. They must always be determined to sort them as failing to do so can disrupt progress. Students now live in a world where all information is readily available online. Senior students can access this information themselves while younger ones can do so with the help of their parents or older siblings. There is nothing that can't be sorted or solved if they have the mindset to do it.

Problems/difficulties can be recorded in the 'work in progress' notebook and dealt with when possible. Again, prioritising will be necessary. Some problems/difficulties will be more critical and will need to be addressed as a matter of urgency. Also, students will have to cope with setbacks from time to time. An example would be missing school time through illness. Each student, with the help of their parents, must be proactive in making sure that the damage is minimised as a result of the absence. They need to find out what they missed, get whatever notes was given out in their absence and be prepared to do the necessary catch-up work.

Ongoing monitoring of progress

It is one thing having the best overall plan in place, it is another thing knowing that it continues to work moving forward. Regular checks must take place to make sure that it continues to work. There are many ways that this can be done – a student must be their own toughest critic.

I sometimes get my students to grade the quality of the work that they do in a particular session. If they are looking for a H1 or an A in a subject, then the quality of their work must be of this standard on a consistent basis. How am I doing in class tests? What comments are teachers making about my work? What are my parents saying? What are my close friends saying? We must always be prepared to listen and, more importantly, hear what is being said. Don't be afraid to take constructive criticism from those who have our best interests at heart. We must always be prepared to heed any warning signs. Changes must be made to address weak areas. Remember, plans/work schedules are not written in stone. Things must be tweaked if they lead to a better overall plan.

The 'weaker' subjects concept

I always put a big emphasis on trying to improve a little in weaker areas. We can sometimes just accept that we are weak at something and leave it at that. I don't subscribe to this. I believe we can improve at everything if we are determined to do this. I am not saying we can become extremely good at something we are currently weak at. What I am saying is that we can improve a little by addressing the weak area. This might make a difference at the end of the day in the overall context of things.

The same can apply to 'weaker' subjects. I get every student I work with to nominate their two 'weaker' subjects. This doesn't mean that the student is weak at them. It just means that they may be a little behind in them relative to the other subjects. We would do this at the beginning of the year and review regularly through the year. What the two 'weaker' subjects are might vary during the year. I believe that, if you can keep your two 'weaker' subjects as strong as they can possibly be and don't neglect the other subjects in the process, you stand the best chance of realising your potential overall. This has to be watched consistently throughout the year.

Finally, my hope is that students and parents will get something out of this book that will add value to what the student is already doing. I have been over 40 years thinking about this and twelve years putting it into practice in real situations with my One2One students. I have now reached the stage where I am confident that it is close to the finished article at this point in time. This doesn't mean that I won't introduce new ideas moving forward. We must always be prepared to embrace change to improve things. I have always been passionate about everything associated with second-level education and, in particular, working with second-level students. I am still learning! The day I think I know it all is the day I will become bad at what I am doing. I hope this book will give many more students and parents the benefit of my 50 years involved in second-level education.